# HERE

# I AM

# AGAIN,

# LORD

# HERE

Confessions
*of* a Slow
Learner

# I AM

# AGAIN,

# LORD

## CAROLE MAYHALL

WATERBROOK
PRESS

HERE I AM AGAIN, LORD
PUBLISHED BY WATERBROOK PRESS
5446 North Academy Boulevard, Suite 200
Colorado Springs, Colorado 80918
*A division of Random House, Inc.*

Details and names in some anecdotes and stories have been changed to protect the identities of the persons involved.

ISBN 1-57856-263-5

Library of Congress Cataloging-in-Publication Data
Mayhall, Carole.
    Here I am again, Lord : confessions of a slow learner / Carole Mayhall.—1st ed.
       p.   cm.
    ISBN 1-57856-263-5
    1. Christian life. 2. Mayhall, Carole. I. Title.
    BV5401.2.M4244   1999
    248.4—dc21                         99-33835
                                        CIP

Printed in the United States of America
2000—First Edition

10 9 8 7 6 5 4 3 2 1

TO JEANIE,

*a special friend*
*who challenges me with her faith,*
*encourages me by her life,*
*and blesses me through her spirit.*

# CONTENTS

CONTENTS

# ACKNOWLEDGMENTS

It's a common thing for authors to acknowledge and thank two people in particular: their spouses, if they're married, and their editors. There's a reason for this: Most of us couldn't get along without either of them! I surely couldn't have.

So I want to say thanks to my friend/husband Jack. You encouraged me when I was discouraged; you championed me when I was down; you put up with my periodic irritability when this book refused to jell; you were patient, kind, and loving, and there's no way this book could have happened without you.

And to Liz Heaney, my editor, I extend my great appreciation. You helped and honed, prodded and proposed, fractured and focused this book until the last revision was far better than the original manuscript. Thanks for being "tough and tender" and a giant help through the whole process.

To all those at WaterBrook Press…thanks for having faith in me. I appreciate you all!

# HERE I AM AGAIN, LORD

I identify with the prayer, "Oh God of second chances and new beginnings, here I am again." I couldn't count the number of times I've prayed, "Come again, Lord?" about some spiritual lesson I've known in my head but needed to embrace more completely in my heart.

Just when I think, *Well, I've learned that one,* I get a midcourse correction. Sometimes the lesson is one I've misunderstood; other times God wants to deepen my understanding; still other times I simply need to be reminded about it, once again. Sometimes I get discouraged, thinking I should have learned a particular lesson eons ago. But my Father doesn't seem to mind. He is everlastingly patient with me, and so the lessons come…and come…and come again.

I've written other books for other people, but this one is for me. You see, I'm supposed to be experienced. Sure of myself. Confident. Knowledgeable. Wise. At this stage of life, I'm supposed to be relaxed. Instead, I often feel like little Much-Afraid in the book *Hinds' Feet on High Places.* Oh, I may look together on the outside. But inside? That's a different story.

This year the Father gave me a for-the-rest-of-my-life verse: "You whom I have upheld since you were conceived, and have carried since your birth. Even to your old age and gray hairs I am he, I am he who will sustain you. I have made you and I will carry you; I will sustain you and I will rescue you" (Isaiah 46:3-4).

Often I tell the Lord, "This task is too big for me. I'm inadequate."

He replies, "Yes, but I will uphold you."

I cry, "Help!"

He responds, "I will rescue you."

I say, "I'm so weary."

He answers, "I will sustain you."

I lament, "I'm afraid of what the future holds."

He assures me, "You'll face nothing alone. I will uphold you. I will sustain you. Yes, I will carry you until you are home at last—safe in my arms. You may rest secure, my child."

Please, Father, help me remember!

This book addresses two overarching questions I've found myself asking throughout the decades I've been a Christian:

"Lord, will I ever know in my heart what I know in my head?"

"Am I becoming more like You?"

My prayer is that as you read about some of my struggles and joys, you will find help, hope, and encouragement. If you sometimes question whether you'll ever "get it," may you realize that you're normal. Spiritual growth takes a lifetime, and it often feels like two steps forward, three steps back. If you're disheartened, may this book hearten you; if you're confused, may you find clarity; if you're uptight and fearful, may God untangle your fears and make you calm and content. And may you always remember (and, Lord, help me remember too) that it's okay to pray, "Remind me again, Lord; it seems I'm a slow learner."

Power and might are in your hand, and no one can withstand you.

2 CHRONICLES 20:6

# PART ONE

# Will I Ever Believe in My Heart
# What I Know in My Head?

*You are for me, Lord!*
*How wonderful!*
*You are on my side!*
*That's security.*
*Men can't hurt me,*
*destroy me,*
*or even frustrate me.*
*Fear has no place in*
*my heart*
*my life*
*my thoughts.*
*I can say that with my mind,*
*but my heart hasn't caught up.*
*So help me, Lord.*
*Not just in knowing it with my head*
*but in feeling it with my heart.*

# Chapter 1

# "He Loves Me"

*God's Love*

We sat on the covered patio deck, sipping Diet Pepsi. A breeze—just enough to bring a pool of cool to the warm summer day—ruffled the bright pansies in the clay pot at my side. There was a moment of quiet and then Ruth said, "He..." She hesitated and then plunged ahead: "He loves me."

I stared, startled. "How do you know?" I asked.

She smiled. "He told me!"

I thought, *Incredible! Not that Fred loves you...and I'm delighted that he does...but that it happened so quickly...*

A year after my sister Joye died of cancer, her husband, Fred, came out to Colorado to work for the summer. He'd told me a number of times that though he wanted to be friends and socialize with members of the opposite sex, he wasn't ready to get serious. So when I suggested he take out Ruth, a dear widowed friend, just for fun, he did. After only a few weeks, however, it appeared Ruth was seriously interested in Fred. I was afraid she might get hurt. I had invited her over that August afternoon to remind her of Fred's mind-set and intentions. It was at that point she'd dropped the news, "He loves me."

It's quite a leap from being "friends" to being in love. To being interested casually and socially in a few women to being *personally* interested in Ruth. I was thrilled and apprehensive all at once at the suddenness of this development.

"Well, I guess I don't have to warn you that he just wants to be 'friends' then," I laughed. "I guess you're beyond *that* point." And I gave my friend a big hug.

Four months later as huge snowflakes fell, my husband, Jack, performed the wedding ceremony in the presence of a large number of family and friends. Ruth and Fred have been happily married for a number of years now.

*Personally interested* are special words. They are wonderful when they describe the relationship between a man and a woman, but even more wonderful when they describe God's care for each of His children.

And God *is* personally interested in each one of us. His Word says so! "You can throw the whole weight of your anxieties on him, for you are his *personal concern*" (1 Peter 5:7, Phillips, emphasis mine).

Aren't you glad that when God looks at the world, He doesn't see billions of gnat-sized specks? Instead, when God looks at His world, He sees each one of His human creations as a beloved, unique, and special person. Though God has a host of children, His care and concern are so personal that it's as though each of us is His only one. Incredible as it may sound, He loves me so much that if I'd been the only sinful person in the world, Christ would have died just for me! He can't love me any more than He does, because He loves me completely. And He can't love me any less, either, because I'm wrapped in the righteousness of Christ. When God looks at me, He sees His Son, and then He sees me hidden in Christ.[1]

But you know what? Even knowing all these wondrous promises in Scripture, I sometimes don't *feel* loved. I forget how God sees me. I need Him to remind me again…and again.

Have you ever had days when it seems that everything you brush up against breaks, turns out wrong, needs work, or gets in someone else's way? Those are the days I tend to feel "not loved." There are times I get so down on myself that I think, *HOW could God ever love the likes of me?* I don't like myself, so I don't think anyone—especially God—could like me either. When others ignore me, I wonder if God ever ignores me too. When I feel I've failed miserably at some job, when I compare myself to others, when I've been in an ugly mood all day and know it, I'm inclined to feel "not loved."

I'm so grateful that God graciously reminds me of how He feels about me—that He wraps me up tightly in His Word so I can continue to grow in that secure and wonderful knowledge.

One day I wrote:

> *Oh, Father,*
> > *When I look at me...*
> > > *as I think people look*
> > > *at me (a getting-older woman, a housewife)*
> > *I see*
> > > *an appendage on the Body*
> > > *valueless*
> > > *one that most people put up with*
> > > > *but wouldn't much care if it*
> > > > *weren't present to bother with.*
> > *But when I look at me*
> > > *through Your eyes,*
> > > *as I see You*
> > > *in Your Word,*
> > *I see myself valued,*
> > > *treasured by You*
> > > *as an integral part of Your body.*
>
> *O God,*
> > *Help my meditations to be on You*
> > *and not on people*

*or how they think—*
*or how I think they think!*
*Every day make Your viewpoint*
*a bit clearer to me.*
*You understand.*
*You know what is best for me*
*at all times...*
*And You care.*

*Thank You.*

My mind can't comprehend why—but I am so grateful it's true: He loves me! And He loves you just the same.

By day the LORD directs his love,
at night his song is with me.

PSALM 42:8

Chapter 2

# BLOBBING

*God's Love*

I was tired after two packed days…four flights (two on a tiny plane), one night in a strange bed, a hurried trip to a small airport, and three hours waiting for my connection in Chicago's O'Hare. At last my flight was announced: "First class passengers rows one to four, please board."

I glanced at my boarding pass and saw it was stamped 4A. *Strange.* Most planes I fly on have only two rows of first class. *The announcement must have been a mistake,* I thought. But I boarded as directed.

And there was my seat—in first class! The section did have four rows, and I was in 4A.

I sat my carry-on down and made my way upstream past the oncoming passengers to the flight attendant who was taking the boarding passes.

"Excuse me," I said. "I think there's been a mistake. I have 4A, but 4A is in first class instead of coach. What should I do?"

I detected a twinkle in his eye as he responded, "If I were you, I'd sit down, be quiet, and enjoy."

I did just that!

As the plane lifted off from O'Hare and the sparkling lights of the city appeared beneath us, I thought, *What serendipity! But it's also pure grace. I didn't expect it. I didn't pay for it. I didn't ask for it. And I certainly don't deserve it! What a picture of God's grace and care for me!*

Since early childhood, I've been reminded of the saying, "The hurrier I go, the behinder I get," and I've needed the reminder! My mind races long after my body has completed its tasks for the day. When I turn off the bedside lamp at night, my body may say, "Good night," but my mind looks around wide-eyed and chirps, "Well, hello there!" I have difficulty being quiet long enough to simply *enjoy* God's love for me.

My family tells me I need to learn to *blob,* a term I once saw in a Peanuts cartoon. A disgusted Lucy tells a relaxed Linus (who's collapsed into a beanbag chair in front of the TV) that he isn't doing anything. He's just sitting there like a blob. Linus nods and says, "That's it, Lucy! That's what I'm doing. I'm blobbing!"

*Blobbing* is doing nothing very slowly. And sometimes we *need* to blob. Our bodies need it. Our minds need it. Our emotions need it. Even our spirits need it. At times we need to drop out of the race—even the human race—for a short time and do nothing. Rest. Only then will we feel God's arms of love wrapped around us and hear Him whisper, "Beloved, I care for you."

When the Lord reached out in love to say, "Come to me, all you who are weary and burdened, and I will give you rest" (Matthew 11:28), I wonder...did He have *blobbing* in mind?

When Christ was about to feed the multitudes, He "directed the people to sit down on the grass" (Matthew 14:19). In fact, whenever Jesus provided food for the multitudes, the Gospels make a point of saying that He instructed the people to *sit down.* Christ often performed miracles of healing while the people were milling about or while the crowds surrounded Him on the dusty roads of Judea. However, in order to be fed by Him, they had to stop, get somewhat organized, and sit down. Christ never ordered a cafeteria line. He never set up a fast-food counter. Instead, he asked the people to sit down and be served. That gave them time to chew slowly and digest. To rest and enjoy His loving care.

And then there's the story of Mary and Martha. You remember, I'm sure, how Martha was rushing about, "distracted by all the preparations that had to be made," and "worried and upset about many things," complaining that Mary wasn't helping. But Christ reminded her that Mary had "chosen what is better." And what was Mary doing? *Sitting* at the feet of Jesus...and listening (Luke 10:38-42).

The lesson is apparent. When I sit, I let someone else take over. I need to *sit still* in order to be fed by the Lord and feel His care for me.

The story is told of a weary Christian lying awake one night, trying to hold the world together by his worrying. Then he hears the Lord gently say to him, "Now you go to sleep, Jim. I'll sit up."

So, my friend, sit down. Be quiet. And enjoy God's love for you. It's really okay—even necessary sometimes—to blob.

> Then Jesus directed them to have all the people
> sit down...on the green grass.
>
> MARK 6:39

# Chapter 3

# God's
# "Special Guys"

*God's Love*

I'll never forget the first time God performed a miracle, just for Jack and me.

I had a giant DRA ("Dirty Rotten Attitude")—and with good reason! It was more than my PMS and cramps. We had just received a bill, stamped with large letters OVERDUE. Only mildew and dust resided in our bank account—nothing close to the $19.25 we owed. Depression hung over our house trailer like a black cloud.

Lying on the bed, doubled over with a heating pad on my stomach, I felt miserable. How were we going to pay this overdue bill? How were we going to eat? I was working full-time for a finance company—at a job I hated—to try to support Jack through seminary. He was working part-time as a night watchman at a factory. But even with two incomes, we couldn't meet our expenses. We had cut out all extras—we didn't have a telephone, didn't subscribe to the newspaper, rarely ate out. Our "dates" consisted of going to a large department store, holing up in a booth, and listening to some 45 RPM records. Occasionally we'd buy one for fifty cents. (You can tell this was a LONG time ago!)

"Lord," I moaned. "I don't know what else we can do. This bill needs paying. We don't get a paycheck for another couple of weeks, and even when we do, it's already spoken for. We need help!"

A few minutes later, I heard Jack open the door. He walked the few steps to the bedroom (our trailer was only twenty-eight feet long) and without a word, handed me an envelope. I stared in wonder at the twenty-dollar bill it contained. No note. Just twenty dollars.

"But who…?" I stammered.

Jack grinned. "I don't know, honey. I don't know who sent it or where it came from. It just appeared in our mailbox this afternoon."

Wonder and joy filled my heart. God knew! And He responded! Right then and there, He had performed a small miracle just for us…to remind us that He cared.

It wasn't the last time, of course. During those four years of graduate school, God supplied our needs in many unusual ways. But I'll never forget the first time the wonderful truth penetrated my heart: *I'm special to God, and He cares for me—not because I'm deserving, but because I'm His child.*

I once heard a story about a father who was tucking his six-year-old in for the night. The father asked his child, "Son, when does Daddy love you the most? When you've been fighting with your sister and getting into a lot of trouble? Or when you've been helpful to Mommy and real nice to everyone?"

The son thought for a moment and then responded confidently, "Both times!"

"Right," the father said, "and do you know why?"

"'Cause I'm your special guy."

That was his daddy's nickname for him: "Daddy's Special Guy." The boy knew his daddy loved him no matter what because he was Daddy's Special Guy.

That child had grasped a truth that you and I sometimes fail to understand: *There is no limit to God's love.* F. B. Meyer said that God's love is in so great supply that it's like the Amazon River flowing down to water one daisy.

That means I never have to wonder if God knows how I'm feeling. He does.

I never have to ask if God knows what I'm thinking. He does.

I never have to think, *Does He understand?* Because yes, He does! My life holds no surprises for Him. He's known all about it from eternity past.

Whether through twenty dollars tucked in an envelope in response to a desperate cry, or through the mundane events of every day, God continually demonstrates His personal interest and love for us—simply because we are His children, His "special guys."

Praise be to the God and Father of our Lord Jesus Christ,
who has blessed us in the heavenly realms
with every spiritual blessing in Christ.

EPHESIANS 1:3

# Chapter 4

# AMAZING GRACE

*God's Love*

I left a Post-It note on the checkbook, with a picture of a sad face and the words, "Sorry! I goofed!" I'd mixed up the check numbers, the amounts, and the balance. The page was a mess of crossed-out lines and corrections.

Jack worked on the checkbook just before bedtime, and came into the bedroom chuckling. "If you think that page was messy, you should see the one before. I completely fouled it up by subtracting instead of adding one hundred twenty dollars."

As I leaned over to kiss him (and thank him!), I again breathed a prayer of thanks for a husband who accepts and loves me, warts and all. But Jack does far more than that. He believes in me. He champions me. Every day I feel his approval, appreciation, and encouragement. He's the president of my fan club. He marches at the head of my parade. He roots for me loudly and cheers me on when the going gets tough. The gift of his faithful love is priceless.

Yet as much as Jack demonstrates his love by understanding and accepting me, God demonstrates His love even more. He doesn't even remember my failures. He only recalls—and celebrates—my victories. And He has been doing that throughout the history of the human race. Just ask Gideon.[1]

It's night, and Gideon is threshing wheat. He mumbles to himself, "Curse those Midianites! They steal everything from God's people—our crops, our livestock, until now we have nothing! We hide in caves and in clefts in the mountains, but they still find us. And here I am trying to hide my threshing by doing it in a wine-press so they won't get my wheat. Things are about as bad as they can be!"

Suddenly the angel of the Lord appears and says, "The Lord is with you, mighty warrior."

*Mighty warrior?* Gideon looks around to see who the angel is talking to, but no one is there but him. Then Gideon starts to protest, argue, and accuse the Lord of abandoning His people. But the Lord isn't deterred. He commands Gideon to go and save Israel from its Midianite enemies. Then He adds, "Am *I* not sending you?"

"You've got to be kidding, Lord!" Gideon protests. "You've got to know that my tribe is the least of all the tribes, my family the least in the tribe, and I the least in my family! No way could I do that!"

God says, "I will be with you and you will strike down all the Midianites together."

"But Lord…"

"You!"

"Well, maybe…but I'll need some assurance that it's really You telling me to do this."

"Fine," says the Lord. "What sign would you like?" Then God orchestrates a series of miraculous events to convince Gideon that He has spoken. But Gideon is still terrified to lead his meager troops into battle against the powerful Midianites.

God, ever patient and gracious, tells Gideon that if he is still afraid, he can sneak down to the enemy camp with his servant. When he does, he overhears an enemy discussing a dream and another enemy inter-preting the dream. The interpretation reveals that Gideon is going to win the battle against the Midianites. His confidence renewed, Gideon rushes back to his men shouting, "Let's attack!"

That scene amazes me. Gideon believed the enemy when he didn't believe God Himself! But what is even more amazing is that God understood and accepted Gideon's human frailty. God even used it to encourage, strengthen, and direct Gideon. And God used him to save His people.

After all that I would have thought Gideon would be remembered as a fearful man who needed all kinds of reassurance before being willing to face his enemies. But that's not the case. Instead, he is listed in Hebrews 11's "hall of fame" and called a "brave warrior" in the book of Judges. That, my friend, is God's amazing grace and love!

Years ago Jack and I experienced a season when we felt like failures on every front. We had four men and a couple living with us for discipleship training. One man turned against us, causing the others to become critical of us as well. We were reproached for everything from our personal ministry to our leadership—and even our relationship with each other. We felt as though we were no good at all to the organization we served, and we were on the verge of resigning from the Navigators. Then God did something for us like He did for Gideon.

Before sending in his resignation letter, Jack spent forty-eight hours by himself to pray and ask direction from God. Instead of directing Jack to quit, God gave him the idea to begin something entirely new within the organization.

"But, Lord," Jack protested, "I feel as though I've failed in the job I'm doing. How can I presume to take on even greater responsibility?" (Sound familiar? "My tribe is the least of all tribes, and my family is the least of my tribe, and I'm the least in my family.")

But in prayer Jack only became more convinced of what God had laid on his heart. When Jack told me that he believed this was what God wanted us to do, we both panicked.

"Are you sure?" I asked.

"As sure as I've ever been," was Jack's response.

But we, like Gideon, needed reassurance that it was God's voice Jack had heard.

As we talked and prayed, we knew that to follow the directions Jack believed he'd received, three things were necessary: enough money to fly to California and talk with his boss (our bank account currently had a zero balance); a low-fare, last-minute airline ticket (unheard of!); and a free day in his supervisor's busy schedule (also very rare).

Like Gideon, we "threw out the fleece." First, we prayed about the three requirements. Then I prayed, "Lord, if this is really of You, please have Jack's boss right there by the phone when we call." Lee was traveling in California, and we didn't know his schedule. When I looked up from my prayer, Jack was wide-eyed. It was enough that we were going to ask for three seemingly impossible things; now I had just asked for a fourth!

Jack called the home where we thought Lee was staying. When a man answered and Jack asked if he knew where Lee might be, the man said, "Just a minute. He's sitting right here." Lee assured Jack that he would make time to talk when Jack arrived. Within the next twenty-four hours, Jack was able to purchase an inexpensive airline ticket with money God provided in an incredible way. Later, as Jack met with Lee in California, God's direction for our future ministry was confirmed.

We have an awesome God! One who chooses to remember what we do right. One who understands our human frailties—our fears, our weaknesses, our doubts. One who graciously reminds us of His amazing grace, even when we least deserve it.

Looking back over my life, I easily recall countless times I've failed—failed to speak up for my faith; failed to keep my temper; failed to conquer envy, fear, pride, selfishness. I have to think hard to remember a few occasions of victory. But God chooses to remember my victories and forget my defeats. His gracious love conquers all my sin. And Jack's. And Gideon's. And yours, too.

> This is love: not that we loved God, but that he loved us
> and sent his Son as an atoning sacrifice for our sins.
>
> 1 JOHN 4:10

Chapter 5

# ROOTED IN LOVE

*God's Love*

I had it in my head that my plane from Nashville to Colorado Springs left at 9:00 A.M. My hostess picked me up in plenty of time, dropped her family off at church, and stopped for gas en route to the airport. As we pulled out of the filling station at 8:10, I pulled out my ticket to check what seat I'd been assigned. I was horrified to discover that departure time was 8:20!

I gasped, informed the woman driving me, and we hurried as quickly as possible to the airport.

Too late! The plane had departed, and I stood at the ticket counter, dismayed and frustrated.

It wouldn't have been so bad, except it was spring-break weekend and every seat on every subsequent flight was taken—and flights were overbooked as well. After futilely checking with all the other airlines and getting on the standby list for a much later flight, I slumped in the waiting area and thought, *What a stupid thing to do!* And it was. Then I prayed, "Lord, help! This was all my stupid mistake, and I need rescuing here, please."

I haven't always felt I could pray about problems like this, problems I've brought on myself, and so I've stewed and worried and felt miserable about being so dumb, rather than asking God for help. However, that particular day I recalled Isaiah 46:3-4 (which I had recently memorized): "Listen to me, O house of Jacob, all you who remain of the house of Israel, you whom I have upheld since you were conceived, and have carried since your birth. Even to your old age and gray hairs I am he, I am he who will sustain you. I have made you and I will carry you; I will sustain you and I will rescue you." God's Word reminded me that He wanted me to ask Him for help. His peace immediately settled over my spirit. No, I didn't miraculously get on a flight an hour later. In fact, I didn't get home until late that night instead of around noon as originally scheduled. But God did rescue me. He got me on standby—a miracle in itself—on *two* full flights. He also gave me a restful and enjoyable day at the airport, reading, studying, and eating lunch. And He had already given me an understanding and sympathetic husband who welcomed me home late that evening.

Early in my Christian life, God often worked in spectacular and dramatic ways (such as the anonymous twenty dollars in our mailbox) in answer to my prayers. Such tangible answers were no doubt necessary to strengthen the weak muscles of my young faith. Today, however, I see the evidence of God's love more frequently in His quiet but consistent acts of care. In His sustaining me. Upholding me. Carrying me. And, yes, in His rescuing me from my own mistakes.

How can you and I feel secure in God's care? By trusting in His deep love for us. And how do we grow in trust? By being anchored in the truth of His Word.

Another verse comes to mind:

And I pray that Christ will be more and more at home in
your hearts as you trust in him. May your roots go down
deep into the soil of God's marvelous love. And may you have
the power to understand, as all God's people should, how
wide, how long, how high, and how deep his love really is.
May you experience the love of Christ, though it is so great

you will never fully understand it. Then you will be filled with the fullness of life and power that comes from God. (Ephesians 3:17-19, NLT)

If we are deeply rooted in the soil of God's marvelous love, then we will experience the blessed confidence that His love surrounds us from every direction...even when we make stupid mistakes!

Because your love is better than life,
my lips will glorify you.

PSALM 63:3

Chapter 6

# HIS WATCHFUL CARE

*God's Love*

I took a deep breath to settle my nerves, but then decided praying was better. "Lord," I whispered. "I'm scared. I've got to drive home across town and the streets are sheer ice. I hate driving in this kind of weather. Please, protect me." Putting my car into gear, I began inching my way home.

The potential disaster happened about six blocks from my destination. A pickup, moving too fast for conditions, slid out of a side street and rammed into the van in front of me. Both vehicles, in what seemed to be slow motion, skidded directly toward my car, and I waited numbly for the crash. But inches from my fender, the two vehicles parted, as though an invisible wall protected me. The pickup veered to the right, the van lurched to the left.

Stunned, I murmured, "Thank You, Father! Thank You for Your protection tonight." The police came, and I answered their questions as the two wrecked vehicles were towed away. Finally, I proceeded on home, shaky but praising God all the way for His care.

As I lay in bed later, my thoughts flooded with the "what ifs." What if my small compact had been crushed by the large pickup headed directly for my side of the car? What if, at this moment, I was lying in a hospital instead of in my own bed? In the dark, amidst all the what ifs, another question emerged: Would I have thanked the Lord if the protection I had prayed for wasn't the kind God gave?

I thought about a friend who had been broadsided in her car by a truck. She was pinned inside her vehicle for an hour and had extensive injuries. Did she thank the Lord for His protection? Then I remembered she had told me that she felt God's presence as the police were prying her out, that she felt His presence with her in the hospital. In fact, God's care for her was so vivid that her relationship with Him only deepened as a result of her ordeal.

God's care doesn't always mean He spares us from illness or injury. But on that icy night, I think He did send angels to protect me. I believe He does this far more often than we know or see. But even when He allows something that we consider bad to happen to us, the truth is that we are always…every moment of our lives…under His watchful care. His love is so great that He never takes His eye off of any one of His children, not even for a millisecond.

In l Peter 1:5 the Lord tells me that I am "shielded" by God's power. Psalm 139:5 declares: "You [Lord] hem me in—behind and before; you have laid your hand upon me."

And that's not all! God is faithful to protect me from what's inside that shield as well—namely, me! And believe me, I need that protection. My life is littered with blunders, mistakes, and choices made in ignorance—moves that could hurt me, sometimes severely. It's comforting to know that my Protector and Defender watches over those things, too!

I remember one summer afternoon when Jack and I waited on the shady side of the Main Street Plaza for Disney's "Remember the Magic" twenty-fifth anniversary parade to begin. A young father, his small almost-three son in his arms, stood beside us. The boy looked apprehensive, and the father reassured him by whispering, "I would never let you do anything that would hurt you."

My eyes met his in that moment. He smiled and explained, "He's afraid of Mickey Mouse. Well, all the characters really."

We murmured our understanding and said, "Our daughter screamed in fear of the department store Santa."

"That, too," he nodded.

A bit later, I heard him say, "Son, I've got to put you down a minute. My arms are aching." But when the boy looked terrified, the father gathered him back up, changing his son's position from arms to shoulders and back to aching arms again for the full forty-five minutes we stood and watched the parade.

I was as interested in the boy's reaction to the Disney characters that rode, danced, and walked by us as I was in the parade itself. Feeling secure on his father's shoulders, the little guy smiled shyly as the first float rolled by carrying Minnie Mouse and Cinderella. Soon he was laughing at the antics of the animals and teacups from *Beauty and the Beast* and *The Little Mermaid.* Near the end of the procession, he was waving enthusiastically at the characters—even Mickey Mouse!

That night as I lay in the quiet of our condo bedroom, the young father's reassuring words edged into my thoughts. He had said, "I would never let you do anything that would hurt you." He hadn't promised, "I wouldn't let anything hurt you." No. His promise went beyond that: "I would never let *you* do anything that would hurt you."

I need God to care for me that way—to not let *me* do anything that would hurt *me!* If I look to God and place my trust in Him, His shield will protect me from outside dangers and from my own silly fears and blundering self.

Does that mean nothing bad will happen to me if I'm sincerely trying to follow Him? No. Sometimes bad things do happen to God's children. But I can be assured that every event that may be considered bad, every hurtful and painful situation or happening, is for my ultimate good—to make me more like Jesus, which is why I'm here at all (Romans 8:29).

I will never be able to fully explore or understand God's love. I think I'll be learning about it even throughout eternity. It is so multi-faceted that millions of books couldn't begin to describe it accurately. God's love is beyond the human capacity to comprehend.

But His voice continually whispers, "Fear not, little one. I am watching over you. Keep listening and looking for My presence. Keep believing in My everlasting love."

> How precious to me are your thoughts, O God!
> How vast is the sum of them!
>
> PSALM 139:17

# TO REMIND YOU AGAIN...
*God's Love*

George Mueller said, "My first business every morning is to make sure that my soul is happy in Jesus." Our hearts should swell in love and praise as we see the depths of God's love for us through His Word. Take a moment to ask God to show you some new truths as you consider more of what the Bible says about His love. (For more instruction about how to do a topical study, see the appendix.)

1. According to John 14:21, what condition must we meet to experience God's love?

2. What was the greatest demonstration of God's love according to Romans 5:8?

3. What are God's promises concerning His love in Romans 8:31-32, 38-39?

4. Read Psalm 31:19, and then paraphrase it in your own words. What direction and encouragement do you get from this verse?

5. What are some of those "goodnesses" which God has given you from His storehouse? What do you picture still being "hidden away" for the future?

6. What do the following verses tell you about God's love?
   a. Psalm 42:8

b. Psalm 63:3

c. Psalm 103:3-5

7. What are the promises in Isaiah 43:1-7 concerning God's care and love? (Remember, in Christ we are a part of "Jacob and Israel.")

8. Read Ephesians 1:3-6, putting your own name in these verses and considering the superlatives. Spend a few minutes thanking God for everything His love means to you personally.

9. Psalm 139 has always been a favorite of mine. Reading it recently, I noticed that all the pronouns are personal ones. At least forty-nine times in twenty-four verses the pronouns "I," "me," and "my" are used. Read this psalm slowly, and list what it says about God's knowledge of you and care for you. Then read it again, putting your name in each verse.

10. Memorize one verse from this section that stood out to you. Notice in the week ahead how God uses it to remind you of His love.

# Chapter 7

# GOD NEVER SAYS, "OOPS!"

*God's Sovereignty*

Jack sank back into the comfortable flower-patterned couch and peered at his leg. He gently pushed his finger into it in several places and murmured, "That's strange."

"What's strange?" I asked.

"Come look at my leg. It seems to me my ankle is swollen."

I wandered over and glanced at his leg—and winced. "Oh, my goodness!" I exclaimed. "It *is* swollen. When did that begin?"

We had recently completed a long drive and had begun a series of speaking engagements, but Jack hadn't mentioned that his leg was bothering him. "I'm not sure," he mused. "It looked a bit swollen after our drive out here, but I thought it was due to three days in the car and standing for long periods while speaking. However, it doesn't hurt so it's probably nothing to be concerned about."

His words made a small dent in the panic that was rising in my heart. But when the swelling continued for several days, I said, "Honey, I'd really feel better if you phoned our doctor in Colorado Springs." So that afternoon, Jack finally called. The doctor asked a few questions and concluded it probably wasn't anything to be concerned about. He told us to check in with him when we returned in a couple of weeks. We relaxed.

After we got home, Jack visited the doctor, who poked and pushed and prodded, and then said, "Well, I don't think it's anything serious because you've had no pain whatsoever. But just to be on the safe side, let's do an ultrasound as soon as we can get you in."

The next afternoon Jack found himself in a cubicle with a technician and an ultrasound machine. He is fascinated with medical procedures so he watched as the ultrasound screen showed the veins and arteries in his leg. The technician began to move the instrument down Jack's thigh, saying, "That looks fine…looking good…still okay."

And then she paused. "Uh-oh!" Even this professional didn't try to hide her concern when she saw a twelve-inch clot blocking the main artery down Jack's left leg.

Things suddenly got serious. Jack was immediately checked into the hospital and subjected to extensive blood tests. He ended up staying in the hospital for five days while he was given medications to thin the blood and to monitor the blood clot.

My heart went into stutter-step mode. One minute I was overcome with worry, the next I was affirming my trust. One moment I was whispering, "Lord, are you here?" and the next hearing His answer, "I have everything under control."

In the middle of all this, our doctor (and friend) told Jack a joke about a conversation in heaven. One resident asked another, "How did you get up here?"

The first man said, "You know, I'm not sure. The last thing I remember is being on the operating table and hearing the doctor say, "Oops!"

We laughed—but after what we'd just been through, our laughter was a bit halfhearted.

I say "oops" often. When I whoof the golf ball from the tee, I say it. When I find a salad in the refrigerator *after* the company has left for the evening; when a knife slips and cuts my finger; when I miss an appointment; when I spill mayonnaise on my blouse...I say "oops." I suspect most of us say "oops" frequently. And we project our propensity to make blunders onto the character of God.

Two days after our new friends and neighbors went on their "trip of a lifetime" to Europe, their thirty-one-year-old daughter died suddenly of an aneurysm. As we cried with them, I thought, *What a terrible thing to happen. What an incredible loss. And if it had to happen, what horrible timing!* But God wasn't saying, "Oh sorry! That one slipped by Me."

As other neighbors were driving down from Denver during a snowstorm, their car was crushed between two trucks and, though they came out with only minor scratches and whiplash, the trauma of the whole day left them confused and incredulous. But God hadn't been blinded by the blizzard.

When a friend who is an air force chaplain failed to get the position he was praying for so that his family wouldn't have to make an undesired move—again—God didn't say, "Forgive me! I made a little mistake there."

A refrain keeps going round and round in my head: "There is nothing *incidental* or *accidental* with God."

I don't pretend to know the answers to the old questions of how much of what happens to us is due to living in our sinful world, how much is a result of our own bad and wrong choices, and how much is directly from the hand of God. But I do know that God is so big that nothing creeps up on Him. Nothing takes Him by surprise. Nothing—not the biggest events or the most inconsequential details—is unknown to Him. There is nothing—*no thing*—He is not interested in. In fact, all my days (situations, events, details, interruptions, frustrations, trials) are ordained by Him (Psalm 139:16).

Have you had to learn this lesson as many times as I have? May we ask God to imprint this truth deep within our hearts and minds, and may we hang on to it with all our strength. You and I may blunder and make mistakes, but God never says, "Oops!"

> So I reflected on all this and concluded that the righteous
> and the wise and what they do are in God's hands.
>
> ECCLESIASTES 9:1

Chapter 8

# "YES, BUT..."

*God's Sovereignty*

I heard a story the other day that made me smile. The old bootblack in the barber shop was a familiar figure with his Bible always lying close at hand when he wasn't reading it. One day a customer said to him, "I see you're reading the book of Revelation today. Do you understand it?"

"Yes sir, I know what it means."

"*You* know what it means when Bible scholars have disagreed about it all these years? What do you think it means?"

"It means that Jesus is gonna win!"

That bootblack was exactly right! God is in absolute control, His sovereignty is a blessed reality, and in the end, Jesus is gonna win! But it doesn't always seem so at the time, does it?

*Sovereignty* is a big word with an even bigger meaning. To be sovereign means that God "makes His own plans and carries them out in His own time and way. That is simply an expression of His supreme intelligence, power, and wisdom. It means that God's will is not arbitrary but acts in complete harmony with His character."[1]

Horatio Spafford trusted in God's sovereignty. A wealthy businessman in Chicago in the late 1800s, Spafford was compelled to take stock of his life when the great fire swept the city in 1871. Wanting to know Jesus better, he decided to sell everything and move to the land where Christ had walked. Shortly before his ship was to sail from New York, he was delayed by business. He decided to send his family on ahead and finish his business in Chicago before joining them.

His wife and four daughters sailed on November 15, 1873, on the SS *Bille de Havre*. One afternoon six days after they left New York, in midocean, their ship collided with a sailing vessel. Gathering her children on deck immediately after the collision, Mrs. Spafford knelt in prayer, asking God to save them or make them willing to die if that was their destiny. Within fifteen minutes the boat sank. They were thrown into the water and separated. Mrs. Spafford, unconscious, was rescued by one of the oarsmen on duty in a lifeboat, but all the children were lost.

Ten days later Mrs. Spafford landed in Cardiff, Wales, and sent her husband a two-word cable: "Saved *alone*."

During Mr. Spafford's voyage to meet his wife, the captain summoned him to the bridge. Pointing to his charts, the captain explained that it was just here, where they were at that moment, that the SS *Bille de Havre* had gone down. It was then that Spafford wrote the hymn that has comforted countless thousands in deep trouble and pain:

> *When peace like a river attendeth my way,*
> *When sorrows like sea billows roll;*
> *Whatever my lot thou has taught me to say,*
> *It is well, it is well with my soul.*[2]

Horatio Spafford knew in his heart that God was not surprised by the deaths of his beloved daughters. Indeed, God had chosen to bring His children home. Horatio trusted absolutely in God's sovereignty.

I can never sing the hymn "It is Well with My Soul" without getting tears in my eyes. Anyone who could write those words when facing the sorrow that Spafford faced has learned the secret of trusting the Lord. This person can confidently exclaim with Job, "Though He slay me, yet will I trust in Him."

I don't always remember to trust like that. Even as I write this, I'm reminded of the many times I've said in my heart, "Yes, *but*—"

"What about my sister's death, Lord?"

"Wasn't Your timing a bit off in that long delay when Jim was looking for a job?"

"Lord, what good could possibly come out of that child's injury?"

My guess is that your heart, too, is often filled with "Yes, buts…"

Two things encourage me: First, we are not alone in our questions. Even the Old Testament saints voiced their doubts. The psalmist moaned, "I am worn out calling for help; my throat is parched. My eyes fail, looking for my God" (Psalm 69:3). And second, God understands my doubts and my "Yes, buts…" The Lord assured Paul as he cried for Him to remove his thorn in the flesh, "My grace is sufficient for you, for my power is made perfect in weakness" (2 Corinthians 12:9). My doubts do not alter His perfect plan one whit!

Truthfully, I'd hate to have the responsibility to either run the world or control my own life. I'm not wise enough or big enough or strong enough to do either well.

But God is.

And I'm glad!

Acknowledge and take to heart this day that the LORD is God
in heaven above and on the earth below.
There is no other.

DEUTERONOMY 4:39

Chapter 9

# LORD, I DON'T UNDERSTAND!

*God's Sovereignty*

I squirmed as I tried to find a comfortable position on the chair. I was only three months pregnant, but it was difficult. Besides, it wasn't my chair. We'd moved into the home of a chaplain who was on an overseas assignment. His two college-aged children were keeping the home fires burning. The son, a biology major, raised snakes in the garage, and a rabbit ran loose in the house.

A sudden movement in my peripheral vision made me jump out of my chair. Relieved to see it was the bunny and not a snake, I tried to settle down to my book but couldn't focus. Maybe a snack would help.

I shuffled to the refrigerator, not sure of what to expect when I opened the door. But I didn't anticipate a rotten tomato. Nausea rose in my throat. I moaned and headed for the bathroom.

Finally, I pulled open the front door and went out into the humid heat of Dallas, blinking back tears of frustration. I walked. I cried. I prayed. "Lord, I don't understand! Jack graduates from seminary in a week. We lived for four years in a house trailer because we were sure we could sell it and pay off our debts from school. But now it won't sell, and we can't leave to candidate for a position in a church until it does. We had to move out of our trailer home and put it on a lot, but it still hasn't sold. I'm at my wit's end. Why, Father? Why aren't You answering our prayer to sell that trailer?"

God's voice was as silent as the close air pressing in around me.

We needed at least two thousand dollars for the trailer. Finally—the day before we had to leave Dallas—it sold for only nine hundred dollars, barely enough to pay what we owed and purchase enough gas to drive our old Dodge to Illinois for a job interview. I tried without success to repress the thought that either God wasn't interested or He had let us down. And I was scared. We were committed to serving God for the rest of our lives, and it appeared that, right off the bat, He wasn't interested in our needs. Had I failed to recognize or confess some sin? Was God unhappy with us? My heart was numb with confusion.

We had planned to candidate at several churches, but didn't have the money to travel to more than one church. Once we arrived, however, God began to show His faithfulness in tangible ways, first by leading Jack to accept the position of youth director in that Illinois church. We didn't need any more travel money than we had in hand!

We moved into a three-room unfurnished apartment with only the clothes in our suitcases and a small stack of personal goods from our trailer home. We had no money for a bed, table, lamps, sofa, or chairs. I remember looking around those three bare rooms and whispering, "Okay, Lord, what are You going to do now?"

The day we moved in, a bed was delivered—a gift from a couple in the church. Within a week our apartment was furnished, and the furnishings came to us in the most astounding ways.

There was a downside, of course: most of our furniture was "early attic"—used and old and mismatched, loaned to us by someone who had been storing their extra furnishings. But there was an upside, too. We didn't have to pay to move furniture to Portland, Oregon, the next year when Jack accepted a job there. We realized that the people in the church felt closer to us because they had helped us when we were in need.

Now I would have done it differently! I'd rather give to those in need than be the one in need. I'd rather have had an extra bedroom for our daughter to sleep in when she was born. Lynn was such a noisy sleeper, we couldn't sleep in the same room with her, so we slept on the Hide-a-Bed in the living room. I'd *rather* a lot of things.

But if I'd had my druthers, I wouldn't have learned the things I needed to either. I needed to learn humility. I needed to learn to receive gratefully what others wished to share. I needed to learn patience. I needed to learn what it meant not to have things my way. I needed to learn how to do the "dailies" without murmuring—to wash a dozen diapers by hand each day and hang them in the basement. (We didn't have a washing machine or a car to take clothes to the laundry or the money for a diaper service). Most of all, I needed to learn that God's ways are not my ways...but they are the best ways!

This lesson was so powerful, I thought I would never forget it. I thought my worry-wart days were over. Wrong!

When a friend is not healed of her debilitating diabetes, when another is not given the job she longs for, when an anticipated trip is canceled, when someone rains all over my parade, I still can become fearful or worried or frustrated or impatient...and, sometimes, angry. I take my eyes off God and fix them on the circumstances. In these times the Father has to remind me again, "I am the Blessed Controller of all things. My ways are not your ways, but My ways are best."

I am so grateful He never gives up on me. I'm a slow learner, but He's a patient Teacher.

Our God is in heaven;
he does whatever pleases him.

PSALM 115:3

# Chapter 10

# The God Who Prevails

*God's Sovereignty*

The phone call came on an icy night in February 1992. My brother's voice choked out, "David...David is dead."

"No!" I gasped, sinking into the nearest chair. David. David of the wry smile and teasing laugh who was my brother's oldest son, married with three small children.

I forced the word past the lump in my throat, "How?"

His voice breaking, Kent answered, "An industrial accident. He was crushed to death at lunchtime when no one was around."

Shock so numbed my mind that I only half heard my brother's words: "...moving belt...don't know the exact details...crushed between barrels..." The next three days were a blur. Shock. Tears. Bewilderment. Insomnia. Grief.

When I read 2 Chronicles 14 the following week, I identified with every single word. King Asa felt overwhelmed, just as I did. A vast army of Cushites decided to crush the men from Judah and took up battle positions in the Valley of Zephathah. King Asa cried to the Lord and said, "LORD, there is no one like you to help the powerless against the mighty" (v. 11).

As I looked at those words I thought, *That's exactly the way I feel! I am powerless to fight the mighty forces against my family—death, fear, loneliness, battle fatigue, and heartache that I can't do anything about.*

I read on. Asa continued praying, "Help us, O LORD our God, for we rely on you." I prayed the words right along with him. But the verse that both surprised and thrilled me was the last part of verse 11, which says, "O LORD, you are our God; do not let man prevail against you."

I did a double take. Surely that last word should have been *me*. "Don't let these things prevail against *me*." But no, it says, "Do not let man prevail against *you*."

As I sat thinking about that verse, it dawned on me that the Cushites weren't fighting against Asa. They were fighting against *God*. And I realized that just as that battle long ago wasn't Asa's battle, the battle against the overwhelming pain and bewilderment of my situation wasn't mine. God not only knew both situations, but He had also allowed them. And He not only allowed them, He was in perfect control of them.

A picture flashed on the screen of my mind: A great army was advancing over a hill, and standing in the valley, all alone and defenseless, was me. I cried, "Help! Is anybody there? I need HELP!" Then, as the army advanced—and it looked like I would be killed—suddenly from the opposite hill appeared a figure so huge He blocked out the sun. So powerful that no arrows or atomic bombs could wound Him. He stared down the enemies who were destined for defeat.

And where was I? I was tucked into His shirt pocket, looking out through a peephole. Absolutely safe and secure.

Along with King Asa, I could pray, "O Lord, you are our God; do not let man prevail against YOU."

He didn't. I was perfectly safe because I, like Asa, was under God's protection. Colossians 3:3 says, "Your life is now hidden with Christ in God." I'm wrapped up in Christ, and Christ is in God. Anything that happens to one of His children has to go through a double layer of His protection.

There were many other stressful events during the weeks following my nephew's death, times I sat silent before the Lord, not even having words to pray. But a peace prevailed in my heart. I was convinced that God was in charge of this situation. I could rest in that fact when I couldn't do one single thing about the painful events. Jesus was victorious over death, and because of that, David was more alive than he'd ever been while he lived on earth. Nothing—not man, not sorrow, not death—no thing can prevail against God! I rested in that truth.

Proverbs 21:30 says, "There is no wisdom, no insight, no plan that can succeed against the LORD." Do I always believe that with my heart as well as my head? No. That's why God has to remind me frequently of His sovereignty. And He often does that through Scripture: "In his hand is the life of every creature and the breath of all mankind" (Job 12:10). "He will cover you with his feathers, and under his wings you will find refuge; his faithfulness will be your shield and rampart" (Psalm 91:4).

So, King Asa, I will echo your prayer often. I am so grateful that we have a God who prevails.

> The LORD is my light and my salvation—whom shall I fear?
> The LORD is the stronghold of my life—
> of whom shall I be afraid?
>
> PSALM 27:1

# Chapter 11

# PERFECT TIMING, EVERY TIME

*God's Sovereignty*

Some Bible stories scream for imaginative reflection. This is one of them.

Time: Several thousand years before Christ.

Place: A small desert village in late afternoon. Two women meet at the well in the middle of the square.

Ramah: "Judith! Have I got news for you! That Shunan—she's hired a builder to add yet another room to her house! Can you believe that? Lord knows she's got the money for it! I heard her talking to the man about the room being for that prophet fella—you know, Elisha—so he'd have a place to stay when he comes through town."

Judith: "You don't mean it, Ramah! She's just little Miss Hospitality, isn't she? Too bad she's married to such an old man and can't have children."

Sometime later, same location, same two women.

Judith: "Ramah, it's so good to see you. Been an age! Haven't seen you since you moved back here."

Ramah: "Yes, it's been awhile. What's been happening?"

Judith: "A lot! You'll never believe it! Shunan had a *child*—and her husband so old, too. It was a boy. Apparently that Elisha fellow prayed for her to have one—sort of payback for her hospitality, I guess—and Jehovah answered!"

Ramah: "You don't say! Amazing."

Judith: "But you haven't heard the best part! Just last month the boy died."

Ramah: "Oh, how terrible! What do you mean that's the 'best' part?"

Judith: "Well, Shunan sent for Elisha and he came, and—*get this*—he brought the boy back to life!"

Ramah: "Incredible!"

Judith: "I've seen him with my very own eyes."

Ramah: "Well, isn't that something!"

Seven-plus years later, same well, same two women.

Judith: "Praise Jehovah, Ramah, the rains have come and the famine is over!"

Ramah: "I am, believe you me."

Judith: "And let me tell you what I just heard. You remember that Elisha told Shunan to get out of the country just before the famine, which was going to last seven whole years? (Sure wish our husbands had done that—what a terrible time, indeed!) Well, Shunan returned home just last week, and to a heap of trouble! Her husband died a few years back, you know, and when she returned, she found that Ahabid (he was always a scoundrel!) had taken over both her house and her land while she was gone and refused to give them back!"

Ramah: "How awful! What did Shunan do?"

Judith: "She and her son went to the king himself!"

Ramah: "Oh, no! And I'll bet because she doesn't have a husband anymore and is poor, the king wouldn't even see her."

Judith: "I'm sure he wouldn't have except…"

Ramah: "For pity's sake, *go on!*"

Judith: "This is the incredible part. When she came to the gate, Gehazi (he's Elisha servant) was telling the king about all the miracles he'd seen Elisha do. And at the very instant he was speaking of Elisha raising Shunan's son, he looked up to see her at the gate! He said, 'Oh, my, here she and her son are now—she can tell you herself.'"

Ramah: "What happened then?"

Judith: "The king not only invited them in to tell him what had happened, but when he found out her current situation, he had her house and land restored—along with the full profit Ahabid had made from the land for the past seven years!"

Ramah: "Now that is downright unbelievable!"

Judith: "I know, Ramah, but it's true."

Sound familiar? I added the names to the story in 2 Kings 4 and 8, but the details are true. The woman I called Shunan doesn't even have a name in Scripture—she's just called a Shunammite woman. But the story illustrates God's perfect timing, evident all through Scripture.

His timing is as perfect today, and sometimes the intricacy of that timing absolutely amazes me. One Sunday Jack and I decided to visit a church we don't usually attend. As we were singing a chorus, I noticed that Barb, who had struggled with cancer for many months and had had a mastectomy, was standing a couple of rows in front of us next to a small, gray-haired woman whom I assumed was her mother.

Barb, who is quite tall, had her arm protectively around the smaller woman in a beautiful, gentle way, as though she wanted to guard and protect her. In my mind, I could see Jesus standing next to Barb in that same way, guarding, protecting, and caring for her through this dark valley in her life.

I like to write notes to people when God nudges me to. It's my ministry of encouragement. (I don't always respond to His nudge, I'm sorry to say!) But a few days later, I wrote Barb a note telling her how I'd pictured them.

One night just before we left on a trip, Barb called. She'd received my note just after she'd gotten the news that her cancer had returned, so she was facing further surgery, tests, and chemo. God not only used my note to encourage her at the *exact* moment she needed courage, but her mother, having suffered a stroke a couple of years before, could understand word pictures better than words. So Barb read the note to her mom, who was encouraged as well.

Was it coincidence that Barb and her mother attended that particular service? No, I don't think so. The church has three identical services each Sunday, and Barb's family usually goes to Sunday school before a later church service. That Sunday, however, Barb's dad was sick and so they'd decided to skip Sunday school. Not only were Barb and her mom in a service they don't usually attend, but God nudged Jack and me to choose to visit that particular church, attend that particular service, and sit a couple of rows behind Barb. And then He nudged me to write a note that encouraged Barb and her mom at the exact moment they needed it.

Incredible. But then, He is, isn't He?

Gods' sovereignty is so great that you and I will be learning bits and pieces about what it means for the rest of our lives. God is sovereign over my months and my moments, over seemingly "random" incidents and events. His timing is perfect in all of our lives. He is in control, even when I can't see Him or understand what He is up to. Remind me again, Lord. Don't let me forget.

There is no one holy like the LORD;
there is no one besides you;
there is no Rock like our God.

1 SAMUEL 2:2

# TO REMIND YOU AGAIN...
## *God's Sovereignty*

Lorne Sanny, the head of the Navigators for many years, once made the statement, "You can't have faith in God unless you have a word from God." He's right. So, let's search the Bible for what it says about God being the Blessed Controller of all things. Take a few minutes to pray that God will "quicken" (make alive) His Word to you today.

1. Begin by putting the following verses into your own words:

   1 Chronicles 29:11-12,14

   2 Chronicles 20:6

   Job 12:10

   Psalm 75:6-7

   Psalm 89:11

   Psalm 115:3

   Isaiah 14:27

   Hebrews 1:3

2. What verse stood out to you in particular? Why?

3. What do you think God is telling you personally from that verse? What do you think He wants you to do about it?

4. Memorize the verse you chose. Place it on a bookmark in your Bible, and each day when you read the Word, go over that verse. Pray about it. Consider ways that God may want to apply it to your life.

5. Meditating on God's Word is a great way to help His lessons "stick" in our hearts. Use the vowels to meditate on the verse you've selected:

**A**  *A*sk questions pertaining to the verse.

**E**  *E*mphasize different words as you repeat the verse several times.

**I**  *I*llustrate the verse in a concrete way.

**O**  *O*ther scriptures. Think of other verses that speak to the same issue.

**U**  *U*se application. How does God want you to apply this verse?

6. Think of one situation in your life right now that seems "out of control." Now reconsider this situation in light of what you've learned about God's sovereignty, and then practice 1 Peter 5:7 (Phillips) which says, "You can throw the whole weight of your anxieties upon him, for you are his personal concern."

Chapter 12

# TODAY AND EVERY DAY

*God's Faithfulness*

Morning dawned cool and sun-splashed, like most fall mornings in Colorado. After a special time with the Lord, I expected the day ahead would be a breeze. Jack was in a meeting all day, so I decided to run some errands.

I went across town to pick up a video project I'd spent hours on. It was to be a surprise Christmas present for our daughter, Lynn. I'd selected slides, had them made into prints, and then found someone who could make a video using the photographs and dubbing in music as background. Finally, after nearly two months, the video was ready. I gladly paid the money and put the video and a copy into my car. Then I ran by the cleaners for two jackets that had needed pressing, almost dislocated my back carrying boxes of books into the post office to ship to conferences, and then went home.

As I examined the jackets more closely, I groaned. All the wrinkles—which had been the reason for my taking them to the cleaners in the first place—were still there, with a couple more added! I spent the next thirty minutes ironing them myself and grumbling at the incompetence of the cleaners, vowing never to use them again.

As I was ironing, I put in the video and groaned again. The pictures were unfocused and the color was terrible. The photographs stayed on for an interminable ten seconds each, and there was no music. I put in the duplicate to see if it had music, and found that there wasn't even a picture on that one! (No WONDER the guy had been so cheap!)

That afternoon I put some potatoes on the stove to boil, went into my study and got involved in a project, and then had a delightful phone call from my nephew. As I was talking to Mike, I smelled something burning and realized I'd forgotten all about the potatoes. Not only were they burned, but the house smelled like scorched spuds for several hours, and I spent another thirty minutes trying to clean up the charred pan. While trying to alleviate the smell by boiling a cinnamon stick and cloves in water, I burned up that pan, too!

Then the mail came. A letter from an old friend carried the news that my childhood home had been destroyed by fire. I grew up in a hundred-year-old Colonial house in a small town in Michigan, and we lived there during my grade school through college years. Jack and I courted (now *that's* an old fashioned word, isn't it?) on the upstairs screened porch, and we had our wedding reception on the large side yard. Though my parents had sold it years ago, when home and childhood are talked about, that large old house with its sloping floors and loose windows and coal furnace always comes to mind. Now it was gone and a hole appeared in the fabric of my memory.

When Jack came home from his meeting, he was greeted by a tearful wife (actually, I'm not sure he even got greeted). But as I told him my tale of woe, God spoke to my heart. "Carole," He asked, "do you believe that I cared as much for you today as I did yesterday? Do you see my faithfulness *today?*"

The eyes of my heart blinked as I admitted ruefully, "I...I...didn't give it much thought, did I?"

"Carole," the Lord persisted, "was I faithful to you in the events of *this* day?"

*What a question,* I thought. I definitely hadn't seen Him in all my mini-catastrophes. I hadn't acknowledged Him. And I certainly hadn't thanked Him for those frustrating events. But, all things considered, I knew in my head that He had been present in my day. And so I answered, "Yes, Father. You have been in my day."

"Then what have you learned today?" He asked.

Another tough question. (Why do I think life should always be fun and smooth?) My thoughts quieted, and truths I forget so easily—and need to be reminded of again and again—came to mind. God was with me on this day when everything seemed to go wrong as much as He is on those days when everything goes right. And I'm to give thanks in *everything,* from blurred video images to scorched potatoes.

Life is difficult! It's difficult because of death, cancer, rheumatoid arthritis, multiple sclerosis, and diabetes. And it's difficult to see God's faithfulness in financial crunch times, job loss, rebelling children, and the myriad heartaches of our world. But it's difficult to see His faithfulness in the small stuff, too, isn't it?

It takes an occasional day of burned potatoes and ruined videos to bring me up short on what kind of faith I really have. Do I believe God only when I see Him rescue me and carry me? Or do I trust Him in *every* situation, whether or not I understand?

The Word assures me that God is faithful in everything. He has said He is, and He cannot and will not lie. Numbers 23:19 says, "God is not a man, that he should lie, nor a son of man, that he should change his mind. Does he speak and then not act? Does he promise and not fulfill?" When God says something, I can *count* on it. In fact, God's faithfulness is so great, it's described as "reaching to the heavens" (Lamentations 3:23; Psalm 57:10).

God faithfully does a lot of things, some that I love and a few I mistakenly think I could do without. For instance:

In faithfulness, He afflicts me (Psalm 119:75).

I don't much like that one.

In faithfulness, He disciplines me (Hebrews 12:10-11).

That either.

In faithfulness, He cares for me (Psalm 91:4).

I like that one much better.

In faithfulness, He keeps His promises to me (Hebrews 10:23).

I'm most grateful for this one.

In faithfulness, He forgives me (1 John 1:9).

And this one.

In faithfulness He protects me (Psalm 91:4).

Blessed assurance!

And those promises are just a small sampling of everything God faithfully provides!

If God tied a string around my finger each time I needed to be reminded of His faithfulness, my hand would be swathed in a ball of yarn! But as I look back on my life, I see so clearly that God's faithfulness never fails. Why, then, does a flicker of uncertainty so often burst into flame as I wonder if He might fail me...*this* time?

Is my doubting just my human nature? Satan's lies? I don't know. Nevertheless, God faithfully continues to apply the pressure that transforms me. While I may get all bent out of shape by that pressure, being bent out of *my* shape means being bent into His shape. And in my heart I can say "Amen"—so be it—to *that*.

> Know therefore that the LORD your God is God;
> he is the faithful God, keeping his covenant of love.
>
> DEUTERONOMY 7:9

# Chapter 13

# THE DELETE KEY

*God's Faithfulness*

I glanced away from my computer screen. For what seemed to be the hundredth time that week, my eyes fastened on a sign on my desk that read: "To err is human, but to really foul things up takes a computer." I groaned as I thought, *Computers may make writing easier—but they don't make my life easier!*

Despite the frustration my computer can cause me, I cherish the "delete" key. What a wonderful little gizmo! With one press of a button, it erases an unwanted letter, word, or document. Wouldn't it be wonderful to have one of those to use in our daily lives?

Yesterday I wished I could press a delete key and undo part of my day. I'd erase the ten minutes of hail that fell and caused our bathroom skylight to leak, *again*. I'd abolish the thirty minutes I spent working at my desk while the spaghetti sauce I put on low boiled over—not only on to the stovetop, but onto the carpet as well.

I'd really love to do away with some of the painful, embarrassing, frustrating, and challenging events my life has contained. It's not hard to identify the situations I could do without! Here are a few...

When I was in high school, my mother almost died following surgery. Several times her heart stopped, and worry, like an ugly vulture, hovered over our home. I saw my father cry for the first time, and it broke my heart. I'd delete those weeks of heartache and pain.

I still have nightmares about the time Jack and I broke off our engagement during my senior year in college. I felt humiliated, confused, and rejected. It would be great to erase those wretched months!

I'd like to abolish some days of excruciating physical pain: the forty-eight hours of hard labor I underwent to give birth to Lynn, Jack's unbearable agony with a kidney stone, and my own suffering from a kidney stone while far away from home.

The two most difficult years of my life were when my sister Joye suffered from leukemia. I'd like to erase the pain and suffering she experienced. I'd like to remove the hurt her family bore. I'd like to eradicate all the tears and sorrow of that time.

Yes, there are times in my life I'd like to delete. Or, at least that's how I feel until other memories surface. Memories like these…

Walking home from church one overcast Sunday morning when my mother hovered between life and death, I felt as though I couldn't stand one more minute of not knowing if she was going to live or die. I cried out to God for some kind of reassurance that she'd be all right. Not knowing what kind of sign to ask for, I prayed, "Lord, if you're going to heal Mom, then please, just make the sun shine." Even before I opened my eyes, I felt the sun! For one beautiful moment, the clouds parted and a sunbeam shone down on me like a spotlight from heaven.

Later I was praying with a group of high school students my mom had led in Bible study. The phone rang and it was Dad. "The doctor said—" He could barely choke out the words. "The doctor just said…Mom's going to make it!"

Now that I think about it, I wouldn't erase *that* time.

And when Jack and I struggled for a while with our rocky relationship, I begged God to show me why I couldn't seem to reach Him. He answered by showing me that Jack had become more important in my life than He was. When I made the agonizing choice to relinquish my relationship with Jack, the peace I experienced was beyond description. As a result of what I went through, I've been able to empathize over the years with many women who've gone through painful times of bewilderment, loss, and rejection. I also remember what I learned during that time about love, forgiveness, and acceptance. Perhaps I'll hold off pressing the delete key on those months as well.

When my mind recalls the times of excruciating physical pain, I'm *sure* I'd delete those events. Then I remember what I learned about Jack—his tenderness and compassion, the love he demonstrated that assured me we could survive tough times together. And when I saw him in pain and knew he needed me, how my love for him grew! When his kidney stone finally passed, Jack told me, "I don't know how, but during these three days I can't even remember, God has changed me."

No, no, I wouldn't delete the physical pain either.

As memories continue to flood my mind, I realize I wouldn't even erase the two painful years when Joye was dying. During that time God wrapped His arms around us and revealed Himself as the God who comforts, the God who sustains, the God who carries us when we have no strength left to go on. My view of heaven was changed because of Joye's death. I can picture her laughing, singing, and delighting in her eternal home.

If I can see God's faithful hand in these events—how He used them to bring about good in our lives—can't I trust Him with the events that still make no sense to me? Am I willing to put all the moments of my life, good and bad, understandable and incomprehensible, into the hands of God, who says His ways are perfect?

Yes, because God's ways and thoughts are higher than mine. The next time I forget, *remind me again, Lord.*

> Happy are those who are strong in the LORD,
> who want above all else to follow your steps.
>
> PSALM 84:5 (TLB)

Chapter 14

# WHERE ARE YOU "PUT"?

*God's Faithfulness*

Judy sold a line of vitamins and religiously practiced what she preached. She had a vitamin to cure every ailment. She did, that is, until she became seriously ill with digestive problems. She couldn't eat or sleep, and eventually all her major organs were close to shutting down.

How could she ask her friends to pray for her? In doing so, she felt she would be denying everything she had preached and believed in so fervently. She was close to death when she finally fell on her knees and cried out to God to heal her. It was then that she experienced one of those miraculous healing touches from the Father.

Later Judy told me, "I guess I'd been believing in vitamins instead of in God."

At times I, too, have relied on something or someone besides my heavenly Father.

I looked to Jack's ability to make a living…until we couldn't make it anymore on his salary. I looked to the security of an organization we'd spent years working with…until Jack had to resign from his leadership position. I looked to my natural good health…until some arthritis kicked in.

Time and again God has reminded me of the proclamation in Psalm 62:1: "My soul finds rest in God alone." *Alone?* my heart questions. "Alone," the Father answers.

What do you and I "rest" in? A skilled surgeon? Education? A physically fit body? Money? Control? Power? Scripture tells us that God, in His love, may bring situations into our lives to show us that we mustn't put our faith in anything except Him.

We do not want you to be uninformed, brothers, about the
hardships we suffered in the province of Asia. We were under
great pressure, far beyond our ability to endure, so that we
despaired even of life. Indeed, in our hearts we felt the
sentence of death. But *this happened that we might not rely on
ourselves but on God,* who raises the dead. He has delivered us
from such a deadly peril, and he will deliver us. On him we
have set our hope that he will continue to deliver us.
(2 Corinthians 1:8-10, emphasis mine)

For Judy, verse nine might have read, "But this happened that we might not rely on (vitamins), but on God, who raises the dead." God deliberately places us in situations that test our faith and remind us of His faithfulness.

I have heard probably only a handful of sermons I've never forgotten. This is one of them...

The small church was crowded as Jack and I slipped into a pew. I listened intently as Major Ian Thomas spoke that Sunday morning on how God places each one of us in a situation chosen specifically for us. He emphasized that we must not only believe that God has His hand in our current set of circumstances, but we must also *accept* our situation. He gave a number of examples of people in Scripture who hadn't necessarily liked the place they'd been put, but had accepted their situations as from God. The sermon ended with some imaginary conversations with biblical characters that went something like this:

"Daniel?"

"Yes."

"Are you the Daniel who is the highest ruler under the king?"

"Yes."

"The wise Hebrew who has risen to great prominence?"

"Yes."

"Well, Daniel. What in the world are you doing in that lions' den?"

"Oh, I was put."

"Put? What do you mean put?

"I was sent. And I went. So…I'm put."

"Paul?"

"Yes."

"Are you the Paul who goes on missionary journeys, heals people, shakes off poisonous snakes without incident?"

"Yes."

"Are you the Paul who has followers in many cities and teaches all over the world?"

"Yes."

"Well, Paul, what are you doing hanging in that basket up on the city wall?"

"I was put."

"Put? What do you mean put?"

"I was sent. And I went. So…I'm put."

"Jesus?"

"Yes."

"Are you the Jesus that turned water into wine, made the blind to see, healed lepers and cripples?"

"Yes."

"Are you the Jesus who can command legions of angels to do your bidding?"

"Yes."

"Well, Jesus! What are you doing hanging up there on that cross?"

"I was put."

"What do you mean, put?"

"I was sent. And I went. So I'm...put. And by the way, *as my Father has sent me, so send I you.*"

Those words still burn into my mind. Major Thomas was *put* there that morning to remind me I am *put* exactly where God wants me. And so are you. Knowing that, we simply must rely on Him...*alone.*

In him we were also chosen, having been predestined
according to the plan of him who works out everything
in conformity with the purpose of his will,
in order that we...might be for the praise of his glory.

EPHESIANS 1:11-12

# Chapter 15

# Up Close and Personal

*God's Faithfulness*

We were renting a townhouse from a Jewish landlord, and though we hadn't met him, he knew we were Christians. I was concerned because we didn't have the money to pay the rent at the first of the month. I kept insisting, "Lord, this is *not* a good testimony! There is just no way this could bring honor to You."

I had reminded God that He had promised to meet our needs—that when He asked us to minister full time without a "regular job," He had assured us He would provide for us. I'd asked Him why He hadn't brought in the money for the rent, but He wasn't answering my question.

Jack had to leave on a ministry trip. I was left with the dilemma that May 1 had come and gone, and we had only about a fourth of the rent money in our account. I agonized over what to do and finally wrote a check for the small amount in our account. I sent it to the landlord with a note of apology and a promise that, as soon as we could, we'd send the rest.

The next week a little more money came in, and I wrote another note with another fourth of the month's rent. The next week I repeated the procedure, cringing inside and reminding the Lord what a poor testimony to His faithfulness this was. Finally, toward the end of the month, I wrote a check for the final amount.

And then came a letter from the landlord. I opened it, fearful he was going to bawl me out or evict us. Expecting the worst, I was shocked to read these words: "Mrs. Mayhall, if there were more people like you in the world, this would be a wonderful place to live."

I squeezed my eyes tight against the tears, but they leaked through anyway. I realized anew that I could never outguess God! But at times I still think I can figure out the solution better than the One who created the situation in the first place. Not only do I tell Him how He should work, I want Him to work up close, personal, and *right now.*

I identify with the children of Israel in the book of Exodus. You remember the story, I'm sure. In order to make Pharaoh let the Israelites—who were his slaves—leave the country, God performed ten awesome miracles: plagues that were visited upon the Egyptians.

But the Israelites didn't live in Egypt. They lived in the land of Goshen and were spared from each and every plague. They didn't get boils, their livestock didn't die, the gnats and flies didn't infest their houses. They may have seen from afar the lightning, the hail, the black cloud of locusts, but none of it touched them. The closest they got to a plague was having to brush their doorframes with blood from a lamb so the angel of death would pass over their homes.

When they were finally permitted to leave Egypt, they followed God's pillar of fire at night and His cloud by day. But even the cloud and fire were somewhere above them, not right in their midst.

However, one day, they found themselves in an inescapable dilemma. The Red Sea stretched before them, and the Egyptian army's murderous breath was on their necks. Then suddenly, things got personal! They stood helpless and watched as God caused a wind to blow and dry land to appear in the middle of the sea.

Can you even imagine the scene? A million or so people are told to walk between those high walls of water which Scripture says was "congealed" (Exodus 15:8, NIV) or "hard" (NLT). Peering up into the darkness, they can't quite make out the top of the wall against the night sky, even with the fire from God's pillar illuminating the path. They squint to see ahead but can only make out the people directly in front of them. They wonder how far they have left to go. Will the liquid walls hold? And if they do, what then? The people can hear the shouts of the enemy charioteers and the hoofbeats of the horses, sounding so close.

Then suddenly they're through! They watch as the last person steps safely onto shore. It's only then that they dare to relax. But then through the shadows they see horses and chariots closing in quickly. They gasp with terror as they realize the Egyptian army is in hot pursuit, traveling across the Red Sea on the same dry ground! Death seems imminent.

But at that instant, the walls on both sides of the dry passageway collapse in a deafening, thunderous crash. Men, horses, and chariots are lifted into the air by the force, then drop hard and sink from sight. The Israelites are too stunned to move. They gawk at the black water. And finally, in that moment, they believe that God really is God. The Bible says: "And when the Israelites saw the great power the LORD displayed against the Egyptians, the people feared the LORD and put their trust in him" (Exodus 14:31).

The miraculous plagues didn't convince them. God's faithfulness as displayed in the pillars of fire and cloud didn't win their trust. It was only when they saw God's power for themselves—up close and personal—that they reverenced the Lord and put their full faith in Him.

But this is the best point of all: The Israelite's chronic faithlessness didn't stop God from faithfully delivering them, any more than my lack of trust stopped Him from providing our rent money according to His timetable. Scripture assures us, "If we believe not, yet he abideth faithful" (2 Timothy 2:13, KJV). His grace does not depend on my goodness; his displays of power do not depend on my believing.

Hallelujah! Great is Thy faithfulness!

> Because of the LORD's great love we are not consumed,
> for his compassions never fail.
> They are new every morning; great is your faithfulness.

LAMENTATIONS 3:22-23

Chapter 16

# WHEN "ENOUGH" IS ENOUGH

*God's Faithfulness*

I hoped my face wasn't reflecting the shock I felt as I saw my friend for the first time since her cancer treatments began. Jane's skin stretched tight across her face, and her thin body showed the ravages of chemotherapy and radiation. After catching up on mutual friends and family, our conversation turned to her disease.

"How are your husband and family handling all of this?" I asked.

Jane's expression was serene and her voice calm as she said with conviction, "Oh, God is going to heal me."

"You mean, you haven't even talked about the 'what ifs' with your husband?" I persisted.

"Not really," she responded.

As we talked, Jane said that she felt that if she even mentioned the possibility of dying, it would indicate a lack of faith in God's healing power. I left her, feeling uneasy about our conversation. I greatly admired my friend's faith. She was a godly woman, and I loved her. But something indefinable nagged at my spirit.

I finally realized what was bothering me. Jane was convinced that God's *working* depended upon her *believing*, and that if she voiced even the smallest doubt, God wouldn't heal her. She reminded me of

Randy Alcorn's protagonist in the novel *Dominion:* "He hoped his optimism was infectious enough to influence God."[1]

I spent the next few weeks studying the miracles of Christ. In some incidents, He healed because of someone's faith: for example, the centurion's daughter, the blind men on the road, and the Canaanite woman's daughter who suffered from demon-possession.[2] But more often than not, Christ performed miracles when *no one believed.* He fed the multitudes when the disciples couldn't figure out how anyone was going to eat. He healed the demonic man who didn't know enough to ask for healing. The man who was born blind in John 9 didn't ask for help, yet the Lord restored his sight. Jesus raised Lazarus from the dead when Mary and Martha and His disciples were weeping in despair. Christ's terrified disciples were astonished when He calmed the sea. He felt compassion for a widow and called her son back to life during the funeral procession when no one had thought to ask. He healed a crippled man at the pool of Bethesda who had been hoping for a miracle at the "troubled waters," but instead was healed by the Man of troubled hearts.[3]

As I studied the miracles of Christ, a simple and comforting truth emerged: It is not our great faith that causes miracles to be performed. It is our great God. And God *always* heals.

However, He doesn't always heal in the way we ask or decide is ideal for us. I heard someone say that God heals in five different ways: immediately (which is the way we'd prefer, isn't it?); through the wisdom He has given doctors (Luke was a doctor, don't forget); slowly over time; emotionally, so that we can bear the physical illness; or completely, in heaven. How God heals is His choice. But one thing is sure: His healing is not necessarily dependent on our faith.

Some Christians believe Scripture teaches that God will heal us only if we have enough faith. They support this belief with James 5:15: "And the prayer offered in faith will make the sick person well; the

Lord will raise him up." Well, I'm no theologian, but I think this verse is talking about faith that is a gift from God, and He doesn't always give us this gift. I base this on Ephesians 2:8-9, which tells us we are saved through faith "not from [ourselves], it is the gift of God." I think the "prayer of faith" is a gift, too. However, even if I'm wrong about the James 5 passage (you'll want to study that one for yourself), I believe God heals in various ways and always in *His* time.

God did heal my friend Jane. He gave her two years of quality life when the doctors had given her only two months. And then He took her home to be healed completely on the other side.

Somehow we get it into our heads that God will love us more if we believe more, pray more, serve more. That simply isn't true. God loves us totally, just as we are. Because of what Christ has done for us, we have met all the requirements for righteousness the law demands (Romans 8:4). And nothing—no thing, no person—can separate us from that love. Not even our doubts and fears.

Hard to believe? Listen:

> Can anything ever separate us from Christ's love? Does it mean he no longer loves us if we have trouble or calamity, or are persecuted, or are hungry or cold or in danger or threatened with death?… No, despite all these things, overwhelming victory is ours through Christ, who loved us. And I am convinced that nothing can ever separate us from his love. Death can't, and life can't. The angels can't, and the demons can't. *Our fears for today, our worries about tomorrow*, and even the powers of hell can't keep God's love away. (Romans 8:35-38, NLT, emphasis mine)

In other words, trouble, calamity, persecution, hunger, and cold are not indications that God doesn't love me! Moreover, my fears for today or worries about tomorrow can't keep God's love away. *God's love does not depend on me.* The ONLY "good work" I have to do to qualify for His boundless love is to believe in Jesus Christ as my personal Savior. When the people asked Christ, "What must we do to do the works God requires?" Jesus answered, "The work of God is this: to believe in the one he has sent" (John 6:28-29).

That's it, folks.

Having said all that, I realize that faith pleases God, and God wants to develop my faith in Him. And I want that too, don't you? But don't ever let anyone tell you that God didn't answer your prayer because you didn't believe "enough." God is God. And He will do what He wills.

That is what He says. That is what He means.

> For the word of the LORD is right and true;
> he is faithful in all he does.
>
> PSALM 33:4

# TO REMIND YOU AGAIN...
## *God's Faithfulness*

This morning I sat on my deck, caught up in watching a flock of birds against the Colorado-blue sky. Hundreds of birds wafted this way and that, like wispy smoke in the wind. They seemed aimless, and I waited to see where the bird-cloud would settle. I watched their wandering for perhaps five minutes until a half-dozen broke off, then a dozen, and then the flock dispersed as individual birds flew off to their own pursuits.

Last week I'd seen a flock of geese heading south, their strict V formations straight and true. The difference? PURPOSE. The geese had a goal, direction, and discipline. Our purpose now is to delve into the subject of God's faithfulness to us as individuals.

1. How is God's faithfulness described or demonstrated in the following verses?

   Deuteronomy 7:8-9        1 Thessalonians 5:23-24

   Joshua 23:14             2 Timothy 2:13

   Psalm 18:30              Hebrews 10:22-23

   Psalm 119:90             1 Peter 4:19

   1 Corinthians 1:9        1 John 1:9

   1 Corinthians 10:13      Daniel 9:4

2. According to Psalm 40:10 and Psalm 89:1, what should our response to His faithfulness be?

3. Memorize 1 Corinthians 1:9.

4. What are two aspects of God's faithfulness that you are especially thankful for? Why?

5. In what areas do you struggle to believe that God is faithful? Why?

6. Take one area you struggle with and place it at the top of your prayer list for yourself, asking God for ideas of how you can trust Him more in that particular area. Ask a godly friend to brainstorm with you concerning this and to hold you accountable in your actions.

Chapter 17

# HOLY GROUND

*God's Holiness*

The doors of the lobby elevator of the high-rise hotel in Jerusalem hissed open. Jack and I stepped forward, and then abruptly stopped. A wide-eyed woman in traditional Jewish dress cringed in the far corner of the elevator, hands outstretched in a "keep away" gesture. She whispered urgently, "Shabat! Shabat! Shabat!"

We hastily backed out, understanding only the fear in her eyes and her obvious terror of us boarding that elevator. As the doors closed, we belatedly noticed the sign to the right of the elevator: SHABAT ELE-VATOR. In smaller letters it explained that the elevator went directly to the twenty-first floor, and then automatically stopped at odd numbered floors all the way down. As we asked questions, we discovered Orthodox Jews consider it work to push an elevator button on *Shabat* (Hebrew for Saturday) or Jewish holy days, and thus it is sin. We wondered if the woman in the elevator would have felt contaminated to have two Gentiles board the same elevator with her.

The next day we watched bearded men in black hats and coats at the Western (Wailing) Wall in the Old City, prayer books opened in front of them as they prayed at great length, bowing ceremoniously. While I longed for those I observed to enjoy the freedom Christians have in Jesus Christ, I also admired them for their desire to keep the traditions they believe are essential. The traditions of the Orthodox Jews reflect their awe and fear of an absolutely holy God.

Just think a moment about God's holiness. Moses was commanded to take off his shoes when he approached the burning bush because he stood on holy ground (Exodus 3:5). (I haven't taken off my shoes to pray to a Holy God lately. Have you?) Any person or animal who touched the holy mountain, accidentally or on purpose, immediately died (Exodus 19:12). The ark of the covenant had to be carried on poles so that humans wouldn't touch it, and the man who did was struck dead immediately (2 Samuel 6:6). Seventy men died because they dared to look into the ark of the covenant (1 Samuel 6:19).

One morning I read of the requirements for the priests who were allowed to minister in the Tabernacle. There was no leeway given in these requisites. The priests had to be men (sorry, ladies, we are OUT!); they had to go through a purification process; they were required to be Levites from the tribe of Aaron between the ages of thirty and fifty; and—get this—they could not have a single blemish anywhere on their bodies.[1]

As I thought about those requirements, I realized I didn't meet a single one! I was a woman, a Gentile from a Heinz-variety ethnic background, and over fifty. I hadn't gone through a purification process, and at the moment I had a horrible cold sore on my lip. And, yet, an awesome, holy God welcomes me to talk to Him.

How? How can I possibly come boldly into the presence of such a God?

Then God gently reminded me. "Yes," He said, "I am more holy than you can even imagine. But I am also your Father. While you couldn't have come into the holy of holies back then, you are able to approach Me now because I have chosen you for My daughter. I sent My Son to sanctify you. Because of Him, you can talk to Me intimately as your Father."

*The Living Bible* puts it this way, "Now we can come fearlessly right into God's presence, assured of his glad welcome when we come with Christ and trust in him" (Ephesians 3:12). I may not be welcomed into a *Shabat* elevator, but as His child, I am gladly welcomed into God's presence.

But if God welcomes me as I am, then why does He remind me to be holy as He is holy?

One reason is that God's holiness sets an unchanging standard by which I can measure my own life and actions, and I need that. God doesn't buy "situation ethics"—the idea that something is right in some cases and wrong in others. To God, sin is sin, and unless I continue to look at God's holiness long and hard, it's easy to become desensitized to my own sin.

Here is a case in point: A number of my friends had seen *Titanic* more than once. If a three-and-a-half hour movie was good enough to see several times, Jack and I decided we shouldn't miss it. So we took an afternoon, paid our four dollars, and watched in rapt attention for a full 210 minutes.

But I was uncomfortable. This PG-13 film not only showed people dying in more grizzly ways than I could count, but it also contained frontal nudity. The riveting love story seduced the audience into hoping that the two lovers would consummate their love by having sex—and the audience wasn't disappointed.

At first I chided myself, "Carole, it wasn't that bad. No offensive sex scene was actually shown."

True. But...

I believe that we are being brainwashed by the media into thinking that things that used to revolt us are actually...well, not so bad. When we are too tired to do much of anything else, we settle for the "entertainment" of books, plays, movies, or TV dramas that contain material we'd shudder to see in real life. And we think little of it.

But I don't want to become desensitized to sin. In order to keep this from happening, however, I need to remember that God is holy.

He has said to me, "Be holy, even as I am holy." When I consider God's holiness, I see the need for a change in my own character.

Someday I will be delivered from my old nature and be perfect—like Jesus. But I also have hope that in this life, too, God can and will change me to be more holy, more like Christ.

Lord, keep those reminders coming…please.

> He provided redemption for his people;
> he ordained his covenant forever—
> holy and awesome is his name.
>
> PSALM 111:9

# Chapter 18

# HEALTHY FEAR

*God's Holiness*

The five female lions looked like giant house cats as they lazed in the tall African grass about twenty-five feet away from us. Every once in a while, one would stretch, yawn, open sleepy eyes at our ten-passenger open Land Rover, and then lie back down to sleep.

"Chipson," I said to the tracker, "those lions look pretty tame. What would happen if we got out of the Land Rover?"

He didn't smile. "The animals are used to the Land Rover," he answered, "but they feel threatened if you even stand up. If you got out, you'd be dead within a minute."

Needless to say, I didn't stand up, and I didn't get out!

Jack and I were enjoying a lifetime dream trip to South Africa, staying three days at a safari lodge just outside of Kruger National Park. Each morning at 5:15, a security guard's knock on our door woke us for the early morning game drive. We had twenty minutes to dress before another knock came. With our armed guard accompanying us, we walked the couple hundred yards from our stone cabin to the lodge for coffee, and then began the two-to-three-hour drive. The guard was necessary as no fences surrounded us to keep the wild animals from roaming freely around the camp (like you could keep an elephant out anyhow, right?). We were not to go unaccompanied anytime when it was dark—either early in the morning or after our evening ride. Those were the rules, made for our good and our protection, and we obeyed them.

Did I feel a bit hemmed in? Restricted? Not really. I'd just as soon not get mauled by a lion or trampled by an elephant or gored by a water buffalo, thank you very much.

We make rules for our children for their good and protection. "Don't cross the street without me," we say. "Don't get into a car with a stranger." "Don't drink cleaning fluid." Our children obey these rules partly because they love us. But more, I think, because they fear the consequences if they don't. Our rules are necessary for their well-being and, in love, we firmly enforce them.

God doesn't make rules just for the fun of making rules. They, too, are for our good. Some of us feel stifled and restricted by God's rules for us, yet often the fear of God is what will keep us from breaking them.

God began teaching me this lesson years ago. We had moved to Long Beach, California, in order for Jack to direct a Servicemen's Center and for us to take charge of a large home where six people lived for discipleship training. I was in way over my head, and I knew it. A couple of months after we'd moved, Jack's supervisor asked him to accompany him on a trip to the Midwest for three weeks. It was the first time in our seven-year marriage that we would be apart for more than a couple of days, and I dreaded it. However, my folks had sent money as an early Christmas present for our daughter, Lynn, and me to take the train to visit them in Michigan. This looked like the ideal time.

A week or so before Jack was to leave, he said, "Honey, Bob thinks that you and I shouldn't be gone at the same time. He feels you should stay here to look after things."

"But I don't know enough to do that," I protested. "And besides, Bob may be your boss, but he can't tell me what to do."

"Carole, I feel he's right. *I'm* asking you to stay."

"Well, that's too bad," I huffed. "I don't want to stay here while you run around the country leaving me here to do a job I'm not qualified to do when it's the perfect time to go home and visit my parents."

Jack just gazed at me with that "think-it-over" look, and I knew in my heart that my trip home the next week was doomed.

Do you know what kept me from going to visit Mom and Dad right then? It wasn't because I wanted to please Bob. It wasn't (at that point anyhow) that I wanted to please Jack either.

I was afraid! I was afraid of the consequences of disobeying God who said, "Submit to one another out of reverence for Christ" (Ephesians 5:21). Truthfully, my attitude was lousy. But after a few days, God and I had a long talk, and I finally said, "All right, Lord. Not my will, but Yours be done."

As the days progressed, God taught me some profound lessons. I learned He could be my very real companion in Jack's absence; I learned He could give me wisdom in doing a task I didn't know how to do; I learned He could even give me joy in the midst of my loneliness. And I began to discover, to a small degree, that to fear God is healthy.

Have you ever asked someone, "What keeps you from falling into sin when you are desperately tempted to do so?" I have. People give a number of answers. "Oh, that would hurt my career," one declares. "It would bring disgrace to the church," another responds, or "My reputation would be damaged." But none of these reasons, as valid as they may be, will be reason enough when the heat is really on. At some point the temptation will look more enticing, more appealing, than the consequences. And in a moment of overwhelming temptation, we'll yield. In that moment of susceptibility, only one overwhelming reason will keep us from falling: the fear of a holy God.

I'm reminded of a woman who told me, "My husband and I aren't doing well right now." Her story was punctuated by long, awkward silences. Temporary separation from her husband because of a business transfer, emotional detachment, feeling alone and vulnerable were followed by an almost irresistible tug to connect with a man who cared for her and let her know it. She had come close to giving in to the temptation.

"Why didn't you?" I queried.

Her answer was revealing. "I was afraid I would lose God's blessing on my life."

The character of God, His holiness, kept her from giving in. In my heart, I said to the Father, "Thank You, Lord. Thank You for her fear."

We are right to fear God's response to disobedience. Scripture graphically describes the consequences. When Jonah disobeyed God, he ended up in a horrendous storm, was thrown overboard, and swallowed by a big fish. When Moses disobeyed God, he was prevented from entering the Promised Land he had spent years traveling toward.

Sometimes we think, *Oh, that was in the Old Testament, in the days when people were under the Law. Today we're under grace. God doesn't do it that way now.* But the Bible declares: "Jesus Christ is the same yesterday and today and forever" (Hebrews 13:8). While God's love has been demonstrated to us by Christ dying for us and justifying and sanctifying us so that we are now His children by grace, God's holy character has not changed.

Yes, God forgives. When we repent, He pardons and washes our sin away. But often we pay the natural consequences of our disobedience. If a woman deliberately marries an unbeliever knowing God has told her not to, she will be forgiven, but she will live with the consequences. If we mistreat our bodies, God forgives us, but we may live with poor health as a result.

My maternal grandmother lived with us while I was growing up, and I can remember times when I was disobedient and she would shake her finger at me and quote: "Whatsoever a man soweth, that shall he also reap" (Galatians 6:7, KJV). I almost hated that verse! But today, I know it to be true. When we disobey God, we reap a lot of things, but one sure consequence is that we distance ourselves from Him. We not only lose peace, joy, and contentment, but we cut ourselves off from the delights He wants to shower upon us.

Fearing God is a crucial motive in obeying Him, especially in the bigger issues such as the temptation to commit adultery, steal, lie, or deny our faith. Sometimes godly, healthy fear is the only thing that will keep us from sin. The fear I'm talking about is not a terrified fear of God's presence, but a reverential fear (or awe) of Him because of His holy character. To fear God is to know that He, while merciful and loving, is also perfectly just and righteous. It's being convinced that if we sow disobedience, we'll reap the consequences of that disobedience.

I don't want to be mauled by lions because I got out of a Land Rover. And I don't want to mess up my life because I failed to obey my heavenly Father either.

Do you?

The fear of the LORD is the beginning of knowledge.

PROVERBS 1:7

# TO REMIND YOU AGAIN...
## *God's Holiness*

In a seminary class, Howard Hendricks once said, "It is foolish to build a chicken coop on the foundation of a skyscraper." But that's what we often do! Our foundation is Jesus Christ. "For no one can lay any foundation other than the one already laid, which is Jesus Christ" (1 Corinthians 3:11). But instead of allowing Him to be the builder of our skyscraper through the strength of His Holy Spirit, we often build chicken coops! Instead of the edifice of a holy life, we erect a sad structure of wood, hay, and stubble.

God has said that we are to "be holy even as He is holy." That's a lifelong building project for every one of us! Learning to have reverential fear and awe of God is a good place to begin. Our question is, But how? To find some answers, let's do two topical studies. (I suggest taking at least two weeks to explore this topic.)

*First week*: Following the outline in the appendix, do a topical study on God's holiness.

*Second week*: Zero in on one of the crucial reasons to obey God and become more holy—fear of the consequences of not obeying Him. To do this:

1. Define the fear of God in your own words (a Bible dictionary may help if you have one).

2. Look up in a concordance twenty-five verses that use the word *fear* as it relates to God. Outline these verses in response to the following questions:

   a. What are the consequences of not fearing God?

b. Who should fear God?

c. Why should we fear God?

d. When should we fear God?

e. How is fear demonstrated?

f. How does this apply to me?

(NOTE: This who-what-where-why-when-how outline can be used in almost any topical study.)

3. For one month, put this prayer at the top of your prayer list: "Lord, give me a hunger for You, a thirst for Your Word, a growing awe and respect for You."

4. Take a few minutes to pray and think about the sources of your most frequent temptation. Write them down and ask God for wisdom in dealing with them. Then write down a plan of what you will do the next time this temptation confronts you.

# PART TWO

# Am I Becoming More Like You?

*Dear Father God,*
*Thank You for being there for me*
*when I falter*
*when I fail*
*when I stumble*
*when I don't speak up about You*
*when I complain about Your methods in*
*my life.*
*You are always there for me,*
*understanding*
*loving*
*interested*
*listening*
*aware.*
*You've been showing me*
*that I don't want just to end well.*
*I want to end better.*
*And that means*
*more time in prayer*
*more time in Your Word*
*more time meditating.*
*Don't let me slip back*
*or maintain the status quo.*

*Oh God,*

>   *Move me forward!*
>   *Help me not to be lazy or complacent in things.*
>   *But help me to be*
> >     *fervent in spirit—and more so every year.*
>   *More like You, Lord...*
> >       *Make me more like You.*

# Chapter 19

# LORD, GRANT ME PATIENCE... RIGHT NOW!

*Peaceful*

On my best days, waiting in checkout lines isn't one of my favorite things to do. But that just-before-Thanksgiving Monday wasn't even one of my best days. In fact, I was having a grumpy day. Like the quills on a porcupine, the tips of my dirty rotten attitude were sticking out in all directions.

I brightened briefly when an announcement came over the loudspeaker for "more checkers," and said to the motherly looking woman ahead of me, "Well, perhaps that will help. Which lane do you think they'll open?"

She smiled. "Number three, but I won't bet on it." Then she asked, "Are you in a hurry?" and motioned for me to go ahead of her.

Ashamed, I shook my head and responded with a sigh, "Oh, I guess no more than usual."

She said, "I'm just grateful I can stand in a line that's moving. I've heard that in Russia they have to stand in huge lines and often don't get anything even then."

"I know," I agreed. "I should be thankful not only that the shelves are stocked with everything I want, but that I have the money to buy what I need."

Her smile was warm. "That's true. But I'm in no hurry, so why don't you go ahead? I decided long ago that if I was going to have to wait in lines all my life, I might as well enjoy it." And that's exactly what it looked like she was doing!

As another line opened and I stepped over to get into the shorter one, she waved and said, "It's been good to talk with you. You meet the nicest people in grocery lines!"

*Me?* I thought. *I sure don't feel nice!*

Once through the grocery checkout line, I pushed my cart outside and loaded the sacks into the car. As I started the engine, the radio came on and I heard the notes of a flute-like instrument, breathy and ethereal. The song, "His Eye Is on the Sparrow," touched my soul as I reflected on the truth that God is watching out for me.

*Lord, forgive me. I know better. But obviously I need to be reminded yet again that You are in control of every situation. I'm supposed to be a mirror to reflect Christ. People should see Your qualities in me. Instead, they often observe such a smudged and dirty mirror that they probably don't see anything but grime and grouchiness. How I need Your patience, Lord!*

The fruit of God's Spirit is love, joy, peace, patience, kindness, goodness, faithfulness, gentleness, and self-control (Galatians 5:22-23). At various times, God has convicted me of my lack of each and every one. But the one I struggle with most is peace—peace that comes from patiently believing that "God has everything under control. Relax!"

I'm not good at relaxing! I do housework like my house is on fire. I rush to do errands in the shortest time possible. I shower in about a fifth the time it takes Jack. Thirty minutes after my feet hit the floor in the morning, I've made the bed, put on my makeup, dressed, straightened the bath, prepared juice and hot chocolate, and settled down for my time alone with God. That's my nature and that's okay. But if a half-dozen interruptions delay my personal timetable; if others keep me waiting; if things that should work don't, I'm tempted to feel and act impatient...with the delays, with the people causing them, with the objects that don't work, and sometimes with life itself.

A friend sent this little gem recently:

> I want to thank You, Lord, for being close to me so far this day. With Your help, I haven't been impatient, lost my temper, been grumpy, judgmental, or envious of anyone. But I will be getting out of bed in a minute and I think I will really need Your help then.

I laughed and was convicted simultaneously. Impatience often oozes from the lack-of-peace pores in my spirit. And it's evident, first to God, then to me, then to those around me. I don't want it to be so!

If I want to be a woman of peace, I need to learn patience. Oh, I've grown—I'm not as easily pulled into the vortex of impatience as I once was. There have been weeks when I've put patience on the top of my prayer list (though I wince when I do because I know that in Romans 5 it says patience comes through tribulation!). It's helped to memorize several verses—commands, really—on patience, such as Romans 12:12 which says, "Be joyful in hope, patient in affliction, faithful in prayer," and Ephesians 4:2, "Be completely humble and gentle; be patient, bearing with one another in love." I'm reminded often of 1 Corinthians 13:4, which says that patience is one of the qualities inherent in Christian love.

I want to be a peaceful person. I want to learn patience in my moments, my days, and my years—even in checkout lines! *Thank You, Lord, for Your never-ending patience with me, and for faithfully reminding me of what Your love is all about.*

You will keep in perfect peace him whose mind is steadfast,

because he trusts in you.

ISAIAH 26:3

# Chapter 20

# LITTLE FOXES

*Peaceful*

Picking up my coffee cup, I glanced at my friend—one near and dear to me—who has outstanding success in a field in which I work hard but with limited accomplishment. I'm delighted to be her cheerleader. But that morning as she told me of an exciting opportunity offered to her which she hadn't even sought, my smile froze. Envious thoughts slipped into my mind and took up residence in my heart.

I know better than to be envious! For years I've tried to apply Proverbs 4:23 to my life: "Above all else, guard your heart, for it is the wellspring of life." To guard means to "keep from trouble, control, or restrain." But in an unguarded moment, envy invaded my heart and stole my peace.

Just when I think I've settled this matter of peace, I look up and it's gone. I love Lorraine Pintus's story about her seven-year-old daughter, Amanda, who came home from Vacation Bible School and proudly announced, "I asked Jesus into my heart."

"But, honey, you asked Jesus into your heart two years ago," Lorraine replied.

She shrugged her shoulders and sighed. "I know. But He keeps escaping."[1]

My peace keeps escaping because I forget to guard my heart.

Guarding my heart is one of the toughest battles I face on a day-by-day basis. The "little foxes" of envy and comparison destroy my peace when I allow them entry into my heart. I desperately need God's help in keeping them at bay.

Envy is a companion of comparing, something most of us are prone to do. We start early. My friend's eight-year-old adopted daughter told a lady about the status of her brother by saying, "He's home-grown, and I'm store-bought." Most of us continue this kind of "compare and despair" game throughout life. I heard Chuck Swindoll, one of the top Christian speakers and writers in the nation, admit he negatively compared his voice with the resonant one of Lloyd Ogilvie and the depth of his messages to the sermons of Howard Hendricks. Apparently even multitalented, famous, and spiritually mature people fall into the comparison trap.

Yet Scripture clearly teaches that it is unwise to compare ourselves with others, either negatively (resulting in envy or self-contempt) or positively (resulting in pride.) "We do not dare to classify or compare ourselves with some who commend themselves. When they measure themselves by themselves and compare themselves with themselves, they are not wise" (2 Corinthians 10:12). The *New American Standard Bible* says they are "without understanding." So when we compare ourselves with others, we have neither understanding nor wisdom.

If I want peace to rule in my heart, then I must guard it against comparisons. When I'm not feeling good about myself, I'm sometimes tempted to identify someone doing a worse job in order to make myself look and feel better. However, it doesn't work, believe me. Nor is it scriptural. I am to consider others better than myself and to humble myself instead.[2] Considering others better than myself has to do with humility, not comparison. I compare when I say, "Lord, how come You gave him all the talent and didn't leave any for me?" I show humility when I say, "Lord, thank You for his gift of creative expression. He's the best there is!" Romans 12:3 tells me: "Don't cherish exaggerated ideas of yourself or your importance, but try to have a sane estimate of your capabilities by the light of the faith that God has given to you all" (Phillips).

When Jack and I were first married, I struggled to be the perfect Christian worker's wife. I wanted to be hospitable like Marion, be the organizer and housekeeper that Lucy was, have the speaking ability of Leila, and counsel others like Michelle. One day the Lord sat me down and asked me firmly, "Carole, who IS the person you are trying to be?" I named all the above and more. He said, "Carole, who is the ONE person you are trying to be?" I realized I was trying to be ten people all at once. Then He whispered, "Carole, I've made you just like I want you to be. Relax, beloved. Stop comparing. And be *you*."

When I don't accept the way God made me, or when I wish for someone else's gifts, looks, or personality, I'm really saying, "Lord, You sure didn't do a very good job with me. You're telling me to be content with this? I'd have done it quite differently."

But God says, "I planned the way you'd be before the world began, and I did it perfectly. I wrote every day of your life in My book. I ordained each moment, each event. My plan was made individually just for you. You are unique in the world—in all creation. I love you just the way you are. In light of this, do you really want to be someone else?"

*Lord, I need Your help to guard my heart against the "little foxes" that try to steal my peace. Help me to rest in the truth that You love me just as I am.*

As I do, His peace invades my soul.

> Peace I leave with you; my peace I give you.
> I do not give to you as the world gives.
> Do not let your hearts be troubled and do not be afraid.
>
> JOHN 14:27

# Chapter 21

# "All" Means "All"

*Peaceful*

The Burger King looked warm and inviting that bitter January night. But as Jack and I entered, the lady behind the counter met us with a concerned expression. "I'm so sorry, but the soft drink machine is out of order and won't be fixed for an hour or so. I can offer you iced tea or juice as a substitute drink on our Big King combo." *No problem,* I thought. (And they actually gave us a malt to share instead for the same price.)

As we were about to leave, one of the servers yelled, "BUS!" as a large bus with darkened windows pulled into the Burger King lot. I saw the manager wince and put his hand to his forehead as though to say, "Oh, no! Not without a working pop machine." Suddenly the sleepy pace of the restaurant workers quickened as one girl hurried to clear off dirty tables and two others rushed to man stations at the counter.

All eyes fastened on the bus door. For a moment, it was quiet. Then, slowly, the door of the bus hissed open. I waited for a hoard of people to charge down the stairs and cram the restaurant. But only the bus driver emerged. He shut the door of the bus and walked across the street to Wendy's!

I grinned. All that activity, all the worry, the rush of adrenaline to prepare for the mob of expected customers—all for naught. The Burger King workers settled back into their relaxed pace once again.

While I smiled, I could relate to the anxiety they felt. Often when I anticipate something difficult, it doesn't happen. I worry about something, and it never materializes. I heard somewhere that 95 percent of the things we worry about never happen. But even if they do happen, the God who said to His children, "My grace is sufficient for you" (2 Corinthians 12:9) is in control of the outcome, every time.

It's crazy to worry! And yet I do.

A few months ago I was exercising on the treadmill, and since I still had a few minutes of walking to do, I picked up *Edges of His Ways,* which was lying on the shelf next to the machine. Amy Carmichael writes:

> There are some things we never forget. They may pass out of the front part of memory, but they are somewhere at the back and the least thing can recall them. The word "all" when I hear it read aloud recalls this:
>
> Some time after I heard, and for the first time understood and believed, that we could be kept from falling, I was at a big meeting in Scotland where Dr. Andrew Bonar was speaking. He was very old and could not speak very plainly or strongly. The hall was full, and I was near the back. I could not catch a single word he said, except the word "all." He read 2 Corinthians 9:8, and he put every bit of strength he had into it, so that the one word rang out—*all—always—all—all.* I have forgotten thousands of great sermons but that "all" I have never forgotten, and it has helped me countless times. It helps me afresh today. "God is able to make *all* grace abound to you; that ye, *always* having *all* sufficiency in *all* things, may abound to every good work" [emphasis mine].
>
> *All means all,* not some; *always means always,* not sometimes. Lord, today help us to live upon this "all."[1]

When I finished on the treadmill, I looked up 2 Corinthians 9:8 and was even more astounded. It says, "And God is able to make *all* grace abound to you, so that in *all* things at *all* times, having *all* that you need, you will abound in every good work" (emphasis mine). Wow!

I'd been worried and anxious about sharing a speaking platform with a celebrity author/speaker, a situation which always intimidates me. But with these words God reminded me He would give me *all* that I needed, and that whatever I do for Him is a "good work." Whether writing, baking cookies for neighbors, or sharing the platform with a celebrity! For years I've known that the secret of peace is in a person—Jesus Christ. If, as someone has said, I'm "glued to Christ," if I am abiding in Him moment by moment, I will have His peace. Christ had peace and He lives in me. Christ was "glued to the Father," but even He understood that "by myself I can do nothing" (John 5:30). "Rather, it is the Father, living in me, who is doing his work" (John 14:10).

Without God's help I can't stop worrying. Many nights I've lain in bed, unable to sleep because I've felt anxious about someone or something. I go through an exercise that helps me remember that God is in control. I close my fist around each problem and lift my arm to heaven. Opening my hand, I say, "Here, Father, I give this to You." One by one I turn my cares loose, giving them to the One who is strong enough to do what needs to be done with them.

Whether it's rushing around to prepare for a busload of thirsty customers, or worrying about a speaking engagement, His grace is sufficient to give us peace. Because ALL means ALL!

Do not be anxious about anything,
but in everything, by prayer and petition, with thanksgiving,
present your requests to God.

PHILIPPIANS 4:6

# TO REMIND YOU AGAIN...
## *Peace*

St. Augustine wrote: "Lord, Thou hast made us for Thyself, and our hearts are restless until they rest in Thee." To rest in Jesus is peace. Robert Murrey McChayne wrote: "For every one look at your problems, your weakness, your failures—take ten looks at Jesus."[2] To gaze upon Jesus brings peace. However, our peace keeps "escaping," doesn't it? To have more of this precious spiritual fruit, let's study the subject of peace.

1. Outline the following verses:

| | |
|---|---|
| Psalm 4:8 | Psalm 29:11 |
| Psalm 85:10 | Psalm 119:165 |
| Proverbs 14:30 | Isaiah 26:12 |
| John 13:33 | Romans 12:18 |
| Colossians 3:15 | Philippians 4:6-7 |
| Hebrews 12:11,14 | Hebrews 13:20-21 |
| James 3:17-18 | |

2. Write out these verses in your own words:

Romans 5:1-5

John 14:27

Isaiah 26:3

John 15:4

3. What is God saying to you through these verses? What, specifically, do you think you should you do about what He is saying?

4. Memorize one verse on peace.

5. Write out a personal application on one of the verses or passages you've studied.

# Chapter 22

# FROM GLUM TO GLAD

*Thankful*

She was tall, dark, and drop-dead gorgeous. As Elaine entered our small cottage just outside the gates of Glen Eyrie, the Navigators' headquarters in Colorado Springs, I thought, *How lovely you are! And you're cultured, assured, stylish, educated, sophisticated, and from a wealthy family. You're a cut above the rest of us in this training program.*

But I soon discovered that Elaine had to learn the same painful lessons as the rest of us. As Elaine and I sat sipping coffee at an old and scarred kitchen table, her story spilled out. It's one I've never forgotten, even many years later.

"You know, Carole," she told me, "things haven't been easy for me here. After a few months of working in the training program, I began to feel that the others saw me as 'different' and weren't accepting me. I felt judged and criticized and misunderstood. It got worse and worse until I felt estranged from the rest of the people working here. So finally I took my complaints to Dawson,[1] expecting, of course, that he would come to my defense, reprimand the others for their criticism, and sympathize with me."

She smiled a rueful smile. "But he didn't do any of that."

"Really?" I exclaimed. "What did he do?"

"He looked me straight in the eye and said, 'Elaine, I want you to do something. Two hundred times a day—when you stop to get a drink of water, when you run up the stairs, when you serve in the dining room, whatever you're doing and whatever is happening—I want you to say, 'Thank You, Lord.'"

Elaine continued, "I swallowed a quick retort, and left his office. But a few minutes later, I decided to try following his advice. And so two hundred times a day, I'd say in my heart or aloud, "Thank You, Lord." I'd say it for the beauty of my surroundings and for the mundane things like a cup of coffee. I learned to say it when someone came to me with a criticism, too! Saying 'Thank You, Lord' that many times changed my attitude toward my situation, toward the gang on the Glen, toward the Lord. I trust it has changed me for life."

My thoughts often flit back to that conversation because I'm discovering how thankfulness—deliberate and painstaking thankfulness—can change my attitude from one of grumbling to one of joy. It really can.

My attitude is changed from glum to glad by appreciating what God gives me, by developing a consistent "habit of happiness," and by offering to God the "sacrifice of praise," even when I don't feel like it.

*Appreciate what you have.* Imagine a day when the sun doesn't rise. Six o'clock comes and goes with no sign of dawn. At seven o'clock, still no ray of light. At noon, it's as black as midnight and no bird sings. There is only the hoot of an owl and the swoop of a bat, then come the blacker hours of afternoon. No one sleeps that night. Some weep, some wring their hands in anguish. Every church is packed with people on their knees. Thus, they remain through the night.

Then millions of eager, tear-stained faces turn toward the east. When the sky begins to glow red and the sun rises once more, a loud shout of great joy bursts from thousands of pairs of sleepy lungs. Millions of lips sing, "Bless the Lord, oh my soul," just because the sun rose again after one day of darkness.

God's blessings come so consistently that we can easily take them for granted, killing our gratitude. At this moment my sister-in-law struggles with a serious respiratory illness and her lungs aren't getting enough oxygen. But even seeing her yesterday in this condition failed to prompt me to say, "Thank You, Father, for the ability to breathe freely." I take so many of God's everyday provisions for granted: the ability to see, to hear, to function. And then when I see refugees on TV, I realize I haven't thanked the Father recently for plenty of food, a good bed to sleep in, and shelter from the snowstorm last night and the frigid wind this morning.

Becoming more like Jesus—more thankful—means learning to appreciate what I have rather than complaining about what I don't have.

*Develop a "habit of happiness."* Dawson Trotman gave Elaine great advice on how to do that, don't you think? For the next two weeks, try thanking the Lord two hundred times a day and see what it will do for you.

*Give God the "sacrifice of praise."* Hebrews 13:15 says, "By him therefore let us offer the sacrifice of praise to God continually, that is, the fruit of our lips giving thanks to his name" (KJV). Praise and thanksgiving are easy to give when everything is going my way. But when I'm cross and irritable, when storm clouds and torrents dampen my days, when the world seems downright hostile, when my strength gives out and everything aches, then praising and thanking God is a conscious sacrifice. It goes against my nature. It's demanding and difficult and takes discipline and determination. But because it's a command from God, He will give me His strength through His Holy Spirit to obey Him.

I've discovered that it's impossible to murmur and rejoice, to grumble and be grateful at the same moment. When the bright light of thankfulness enters the scene, the gloom of complaining, muttering, fussing, and fretting is dissipated.

I'm thankful for God's many reminders to be thankful, aren't you? And Daws (in heaven) and Elaine (wherever you are), thank you, too!

Let the peace of Christ rule in your hearts,
since as members of one body you were called to peace.
And be thankful.

COLOSSIANS 3:15

Chapter 23

# DOWN TO THE LAST DROP

*Thankful*

My daughter played happily in the kitchen as I painted the kitchen chairs. After a few minutes, I stretched, rubbed the spot in my back that was aching, set the paint can on a rag on one of the chairs, and turned to get a cup of coffee. In a split second, two-and-a-half-year-old Lynn toddled over to the chair, reached for the rag, and pulled.

"Don't!" I hollered, a second too late. Paint splattered everywhere. On the floor. On Lynn. On me. On the kitchen cabinets. "Oh, Lynn," I moaned as I blotted up the mess with huge wads of paper towels.

A few minutes later as I was washing the paint off myself in the bathroom, I congratulated myself that I hadn't lost my temper. It was then that I heard God whisper. "You didn't lose your temper," He agreed, "but you didn't thank Me either." Then He reminded me of a verse I'd memorized just that week: "In every thing give thanks: for this is the will of God in Christ Jesus concerning you" (1 Thessalonians 5:18, KJV).

"You've got to be kidding, Lord!" I exclaimed.

"In *everything,*" was God's quiet but firm response.

I surely didn't get this one, but I said, "Okay, Lord. I thank you—even for that spilled paint."

God began to show me that if I didn't learn to give thanks for what seemed to be "stupid" accidents—erasing chapters off the computer, blowing tires in the middle of nowhere—I would never learn to say "thank You" for the big things when they happened either.

God says I am to give thanks in everything. That means the happy events and the sad, the momentous and the monotonous, the terrific and the tragic, the pleasant and the painful. Each day I'm given a full cup of experiences—some bitter, some sweet. I am to drain the cup of experience to the last drop and thank God for exactly what He's "poured" me that day.

This morning Jack packed a bag to move to Glen Eyrie for a week of meetings, and I drank a drop of loneliness from my cup. As thirteen women gathered for lunch at my house for prayer and sharing, I tasted drops of joy. One woman stayed on to share her despair over a husband who seems indifferent to her and her needs. I drank with her the sadness of that situation. A friend called to tell me of a baby boy whose heart stopped. He was flown by helicopter from the mountains to a hospital in town, but he didn't make it. I cried as I swallowed that bitter drop. I savored sweet moments later in the day: a chance to share Christ with a recently widowed acquaintance over dinner, Jack's dear phone call before bedtime, and a precious time with the Lord. Today I drank fully—and thankfully—of the moments God gave me.

But I don't have a naturally thankful heart. It's easy for me to let moments of the day whiz by without giving them conscious thought, or to be unhappy about what fills my cup. It's easy to sing of my trust in God during Sunday worship, but sometimes hard to allow the truth of His goodness to sink into my soul when ugly circumstances splotch the landscape of my life.

Over and over the writers of the Psalms shouted out their fears and frustrations to the Father. But their outbursts were always followed by a decision to trust God. In every case the writer said that even though awful things were happening, even though it looked like God had forsaken him, even though the enemy seemed to be winning, he would trust in God. "My flesh and my heart may fail, but God is the strength of my heart and my portion forever" (Psalm 73:26).

This is a hard lesson, isn't it? But our faithful God will continue to give us daily opportunities to drink from the cup of life. In response, may we choose to drain it to the last drop, declaring, "I will trust. Thank You, Lord"—whether our cup is filled with sticky problems, spoiled plans, or spilled paint!

Be very careful, then, how you live—not as unwise but as wise, making the most of every opportunity.

EPHESIANS 5:15-16

Chapter 24

# Count It All Joy

*Thankful*

The morning started innocently enough. I had organized my day and was off and running, right on schedule. But as I left the post office, I searched my purse in vain for my keys. Looking through the car window, I discovered I'd locked them in the car. *No problem,* I thought, as I walked the block to my 10:00 appointment at the hair salon. From there I called Jack (who, bless his heart, laughed an accepting laugh) and asked him to please come with an extra key. I then proceeded to get my hair done.

As I sat under the dryer, Jack walked in, his face grim and concerned. "Honey," he said, "you not only locked the keys in your car, you left the car running. The antifreeze has bubbled over everything. It'll need to cool off for a while before you start the car. When you get home, we'll see what else needs to be done."

Forty-five minutes later, I walked back to the car and tried to start it. Nothing. It turned over but refused to catch hold. I thought, *There goes my morning!* Determined not to bother Jack again, I reached for my AAA card, called to ask for help, then waited another forty-five minutes for them to come start my car and then follow me to a service station in case I didn't make it. Fortunately, replacing the antifreeze and running the car seemed to fix the problem. Plans shot for the day, I finally headed for home, too nervous to get through the rest of my to-do list.

In times like these, it's difficult to be thankful. In fact, it's easy to get mad. If I don't practice rejoicing during the good times, the bad times, the disappointing times, the glum times, the frustrating times— *all* the time—then I'm going to end up angry over the many circumstances that don't go my way. Only I'm not really angry at the circumstances; I'm angry at God because He could have changed those circumstances. To keep from being angry with God, I need to practice being thankful instead!

God continues to teach me more about being thankful, no matter what is happening in and around me. Just this morning, as I was praying for the people I love who are experiencing debilitating illnesses, the Lord said to my heart, "Carole, you've been writing about being thankful and you're learning to thank Me for events in your own life, but you've never thanked Me for what I'm doing through the painful circumstances of your loved ones."

I almost gasped out loud! "Lord," I protested, "how can I thank You when they are suffering so?"

The Lord's silence was eloquent. I'd just written "Thanks in *everything.*"

"All right, Father. Here goes."

I hesitated. How in the world could I thank Him for Jane's diabetes, for Selva's rheumatoid arthritis, for Barbara's cancer? Then I realized that God was not asking me literally to thank Him *for* the painful things in my friends' lives, but to thank Him *in* those difficult circumstances. Paul says, "That is why, for Christ's sake, I delight in weaknesses, in insults, in hardships, in persecutions, in difficulties. For when I am weak, then I am strong" (2 Corinthians 12:10). James tells us to "count it all joy when [we] fall into various trials" (James 1:2, NKJV).

As I began to pray, God led me. "Thank You, Father, that You are using Jane's diabetes to conform her to the image of Your Son

(Romans 8:29). I really trust You and thank You for that." And so it went. One by one, I thanked God for what He was bringing about in the lives of my loved ones who were suffering.

And then something else occurred to me. If we are to be thankful in everything, then does it mean we can be thankful even when we hear news of suffering that is caused by sin? I believe God calls us to an abiding attitude of thankfulness, a thankfulness that grows out of a "settled dependence on God."[1] We can be thankful because no matter what happens on earth, God is still in control; He is still good; He is still personally interested in us; He is able to turn evil on its head and use it for His good purposes.

No matter what the circumstances, we can thank God for what He will do through them. And when we focus on Him in prayer instead of on the difficulty of the situation, our hearts can sparkle with His joy.

Devote yourselves to prayer,
being watchful and thankful.

COLOSSIANS 4:2

# TO REMIND YOU AGAIN...
## *Thankfulness*

It's easy to thank God for our blessings, to praise Him for His goodness and majesty and to rejoice in the beauty of the world around us. But it's more difficult to be thankful during the painful times in our life, to praise Him when we feel challenged and to rejoice when life seems ugly.

Paul Thigpen, in writing about joy, said, "I've discovered that if we want joy, we must abandon the pursuit of it, and go looking for God instead."[2] It's the same with gratitude: If we want more of it, we need to seek the Source of it. So let's look *for* and *to* God as we study the subject of thankfulness.

1. List the verbs in Proverbs 2:1-6 and write a paragraph concerning the progression of these action verbs. (For example, it's easier to "accept" than to "store up"; easier to "turn" than to "apply.") What do you think God is saying about taking the first "baby steps" in order to progress to the more difficult advanced steps of getting into His Word? How do you think this applies to being thankful?

2. According to the following verses, what reasons do we have to be thankful?

   a. Psalm 106:1

   b. Psalm 118:21

   c. 1 Corinthians 15:57

d. 2 Corinthians 9:15

e. 2 Corinthians 9:11

f. Psalm 16:7

3. Read Psalm 107 and list five things to be thankful for.

4. According to Colossians 3:17, when should we give thanks?

5. What are some methods we can use to give thanks?

a. Psalm 13:6

b. Psalm 105:1

c. Psalm 100:4

6. Ask God to put one verse concerning thankfulness on your heart. Memorize this verse and then do the following:

a. Write out the verse in your own words, using personal pronouns (I, me).

b. Write a sentence or two describing a recent situation in which you failed to obey this verse.

c. After praying for wisdom, write out what you feel God would have you do about it this week, and then, if possible, have someone hold you accountable to do it.

Chapter 25

# I SURRENDER ALL

*Obedient*

Even though he was only four, Randy's strong will was evident. When his mother said, "Randy, it's time to sit down for lunch," Randy didn't budge. She repeated, insistent: "Randy, come sit down at the table." The only movement was a muscle tightening in the small boy's jaw. "RANDY! If you don't sit down this minute, you will be punished."

Scowling fiercely, Randy inched to the chair and perched on the edge, muttering, "I may be sitting on the outside, but I'm standing on the inside."

I laughed when my friend told this story about her son, but I couldn't help thinking how often each of us reacts like Randy. We, too, go through the motions, but without a heart to obey. We are like King Amaziah who "did that which was right in the sight of the LORD, but not with a perfect heart" (2 Chronicles 25:2, KJV).

I've seen many women do this in their marriages. Some women are married on the outside but remain single on the inside. I meet wives who refuse to leave their parents or the place they grew up. Others refuse to give up their maiden name, their bank account, or self-gratifying habits. They build walls around sections of themselves and hang "Do Not Enter" signs, and then they wonder why "becoming one" is a distant dream.

To become one in marriage requires relinquishing "I" for "we." It means putting the best interest of the other ahead of our own. For most of us, the switch doesn't come naturally or easily.

Yet, for me, growing toward oneness with Jack was relatively easy compared to relinquishing my will to God. I confess to some heel-dragging in both relationships, but turning over my stubborn will to God has been done in spurts, stutters, an occasional STOP, and sometimes even a shift into reverse!

When I was a child, our church often ended morning worship with the hymn "I Surrender All." I sang it enthusiastically and wholeheartedly, but at the time, I didn't understand what the words meant. I have never forgotten the first time I got a glimpse of what surrendering "all" can mean.

The missionaries who came to speak at our small church always stayed with my family. Our big white-columned, century-old home, with its drafts and sloping floors, sheltered many over the years. Most of our guests were so fascinating that we kids didn't mind sleeping out on the upstairs screened-in porch in the summer or doubling up in bedrooms in the other seasons.

When I was ten, one guest profoundly affected my life. She was a lovely, joyful woman in her late fifties. Her laugh filled the house and her stories kept us enthralled. I remember staring at her left hand, disfigured because the tip of her ring finger was missing. I wondered about it until she told this story...

"After graduating from college, I became a schoolteacher. When I was thirty-two, I met a fellow teacher, and we fell in love. We both loved God and felt He wanted us to promise Him and each other that, should He call one of us to the mission field and not the other, we would break our engagement."

My eyes opened wide as she talked. More than anything, I wanted to get married and raise a family, and I couldn't even imagine making such a commitment. She continued, "Shortly after our engagement, God did call me to the mission field. But He didn't call my fiancé. And so, with reluctance, we broke our engagement, and I prepared to go to India."

She smiled at me and, perhaps noting the horror in my eyes, said gently, "I've never been sorry for that decision. I became the head mistress at a girl's school in India. One night, one of the girls became demon possessed and ran to the well to jump in and drown herself. I saw her out of my office window and ran to stop her. She had superhuman strength, and I cried to the Lord to give me power to prevent her from killing herself. God answered, but in the struggle, she bit off the end of my finger."

She held out her hand and continued, "It took several of us to get her back inside where we prayed for her. We rebuked the demon that possessed her, and he left. A few days later, that young girl received Christ."

I thought about this story for many days after the woman left our home. To me, she had made the greatest sacrifice of all—giving up the one she loved to go to a foreign country and serve God and others. Yet it was obvious she was not only content, but happy—more so than most people I'd met. Her face radiated the joy of the Lord, and I could not feel sorry for her.

Then and there I told the Lord that should His plan be for me to be single all my life, I would be willing. And I meant it. I did, that is, until I met Jack a decade later. We fell in love and became engaged. But the pressure of college life began to affect our relationship, and one night, Jack told me he wasn't sure he loved me anymore.

He really didn't want me to return the engagement ring, but I did, along with his letter sweater, football pin, and other things he'd given me. Then I fled home for the weekend. Jack couldn't stand that, so he borrowed a car to follow me home and ask me to wear the diamond again. But soon the unsure feelings crowded in and we broke up again. (We had yet to learn that love isn't *always* a feeling.) Once more I went home to a loving family for comfort. And once again, Jack and I patched things up.

When he broke up with me a third time, I was not only bewildered, but heartsick. I prayed desperately for God to heal our relationship, but it seemed as though my prayers went only as far as the dorm room ceiling and then bounced right back at me. The feeling of God's presence was gone. I was frantic. The more I prayed, the more I felt the heavens were brass and I simply wasn't getting through.

I stopped to examine my own heart, asking the God of wisdom for His insight, and I gained clarity about what had happened. While all my life I had said that should God want me to be single, I would be willing, I had done an about-face. I was no longer willing to be single. I wanted to be married—and not to just anyone, but to Jack.

As I looked deep within my heart and realized that I'd slowly replaced my dependence on God with dependence on Jack, I cried before the Father. At last I heard His voice in response. "Carole," He said, "do you want My absolute best for your life?"

I answered, "Of course, Father. And surely Jack is that 'best.'"

He said, "Carole, would it make any difference to you if Jack were My second best for you?"

"Father, "I argued, "how could Jack not be Your first best? After all, You put us together. You caused us to fall in love. You led us to be engaged."

God was silent. But then He began to speak again, gently. "Child of my heart," He said. "I love you with a love that will not let you go. I love you so much that I want the very best for you for all of your life. And I love you too much to have a rival for your affection."

My tears flowed as I considered this. The struggle was a fierce one, but finally I surrendered. "Father, I don't want anyone but You on the throne of my life. I really do believe You know what is best for me. It's hard for me to imagine that your first best is anything but being married to Jack, but You know all things. And if being married to Jack isn't your first best, if it's second best or on down the line, *then I don't want it.* And yes, even if You want me to be single for the rest of my life, I am willing."

As I prayed that morning, the heavens opened and the Spirit of God flooded my heart and soul with joy and peace.

It was several months before God brought Jack and me back together for the final time, and another year before we walked down the aisle and said, "I do." But God's joy continued to reign in my heart.

Surrendering my will to God's will in this area was one of the great battles of my life. It was one great big "yes," and the kind of joy it produced has accompanied each act of surrender throughout my life.

> You must worship no other gods, but only the LORD,
> for he is a God who is passionate
> about his relationship with you.
>
> EXODUS 34:14 (NLT)

# Chapter 26

# "Do It for Me"

*Obedient*

When Jack became an assistant pastor and youth director in a large church, I looked around to see where I could make a contribution. Since I loved the group of eight- to eleven-year-old kids and the junior church had poor attendance, I decided it would be fun to work with that program. And work I did! I employed every bit of knowledge I'd gained as a Christian education major, spent hours planning, recruiting, working...and soon we were booming. Fifty eager junior-age boys and girls gathered each Sunday morning. I mentally patted myself on the back.

Our church held communion every few weeks, and I decided that "my kids" should participate. I talked it over with the pastor and got his okay. For four weeks we studied the meaning of communion in junior church. When we finished, I felt those kids knew more about communion than most adult church attendees did.

Then came the big day. All who had asked Christ into their hearts and wanted to participate were dismissed from junior church and filed down to the sanctuary to sit in a special section and take communion, a meaningful experience for all of us.

The following week I was asked to drop by the pastor's office. I blithely entered, thinking it was nice he'd asked me in for a little talk. But after a few minutes of chitchat, he grew serious, cleared his throat, and said, "Carole, I've received a couple of phone calls from parents complaining about your leadership of junior church."

I frowned. "What did I do?" I queried with concern.

"Some of the parents didn't like the fact that their children had taken communion without them being consulted," the pastor responded. "They had wanted their children to take their first communion with the family, and they thought you were out of line to do what you did."

Dumbfounded, I mumbled an apology and made a hasty retreat. As I walked down the hall, anger and resentment boiled on the back burner of my mind. My internal conversation with the pastor and the parents went something like this: "Well, hang it on your beak! I don't have to do this, you know. I'm not being paid for it. I worked hard and now the kids love junior church. I gave it my best shot. So if you don't like it, I'll just quit! You can go back to your dreary junior church and do whatever you have a mind to!"

The next morning, I was still seething as I sat down to have my time with God. But suddenly, God brought me up short. "Carole," He whispered to my heart. "You were wrong, you know. You should have asked the parents' permission."

"Okay," I mumbled. "I admit I didn't even think about it, but I guess I should have."

"And there's another thing," God persisted. "Tell Me, why are you working so hard in junior church?"

"Well," I responded, "I wanted to help the kids."

"Good," the Father said kindly. "But not good enough."

"I wanted to serve the body of Christ, Your church," I explained further.

"Good," I heard Him say again. "But not good enough."

"Let's see then. I was also doing it for Jack, to help him with his job."

"Good. But not good enough."

"Okay," I sighed. "What *is* good enough?"

"You must do it for *Me*."

Then I remembered this verse: "Whatever you do, work at it with all your heart, as working for the Lord, not for men" (Colossians 3:23). Oh.

God has continued to use this verse to give me motivation checkups. When I've done my best and received no praise or commendation, or I've been criticized and I rant and rave over the injustice, I realize I've done it again: I've done the right thing for the wrong reason and the wrong person.

A few years later (with many reminders in between) God ironed out another wrinkle in my thinking. We were about to move into the only house we could find to rent that was affordable and large enough to meet our needs. The house was surrounded by small studio apartments, and the day before we were to move in, the owner decided to turn the studios into motel units and have the people who rented the house manage them. In practical terms, that meant me! (Everyone else had other jobs with higher priority.)

Of course, the cleaning person soon quit. And so I found myself not only being responsible to have someone available twenty-four hours a day to handle reservations, but I ended up cleaning those rooms and the toilets in those rooms. I don't know of a much more distasteful job than cleaning someone else's toilets.

As I scrubbed, I complained. "You know, Lord, I could be doing something much more advantageous to Your kingdom! I could be leading a women's Bible study or talking to people about You or teaching kids in Sunday school or…"

"Carole," He interrupted me, "if I've asked you to do this—and I have—then do it for Me. I've told you whatever you do, do it heartily as unto Me."

"Even *this,* Father?"

"Even this, child."

Suddenly that loathsome task didn't seem so loathsome. God was assuring me that scrubbing a toilet can be a "good work" for Him. I can scrub my kitchen floor, take out the garbage, chauffeur people to the airport—and clean motel toilets—all for Him.

God's lessons don't stop—they just keep coming at various levels on different frequencies. In *Alice's Adventures in Wonderland,* the White Queen said to Alice, "It takes all the running you can to keep in the same place." That's how I feel sometimes! But ever so slowly, I'm learning that my motivation must not be to please people. I must do it— I want to do it—for the living God.

> Those who obey his commands live in him,
> and he in them.
>
> 1 JOHN 3:24

# Chapter 27

# MY PORTION
# AND MY CUP

*Obedient*

Have you had times when you are reading Scripture, and God seems to stop you, take you by both shoulders, look you square in the eye and say, "Take special note!" Such was the case when I read Psalm 16:5: "LORD, you have assigned me my portion and my cup; you have made my lot secure."

I thought about that verse for days. "My portion and my cup" have been assigned to me. Before I was formed in my mother's womb—from eternity past—God ordained both my portion and cup.

My "portion" consists of those things over which I have no control. I had no say in the fact that I was born a middle child of a middle-class family, living in a mid-size town in mid-America. I didn't choose to be 5 feet 4 inches tall with brown hair, blue eyes, and teeth that needed straightening. I didn't give myself a healthy constitution, mediocre talent, a nonathletic inclination, or a strong but not beautiful singing voice. I also had no say in the blessing of being born in a family who had high morals and loved God. My portion gives me much to be thankful for, but I had absolutely no choice about my lot in life. All these circumstances were assigned to me by my Creator.

God also assigned my "cup"—my life experiences, both happy and sad. My cup has consisted of grieving the deaths of my sister and father from leukemia, living with a grandmother who grew senile, and mourning our inability to have more than one child. It's also contained wonderful joys such as a loving husband, a delightful daughter, a terrific son-in-law, two tremendous grandchildren, and a ministry my husband and I are passionate about.

While I don't choose either my portion or my cup, I can choose how I respond to them. I can take a healthy body and ruin it with overindulgence, poor habits, drugs, excessive work. I can resent my ordinariness. I can hate my looks, lack of talent, or status. I can accept both the cup of sorrows and the cup of joys, or I can reject the lessons and experiences God means for me to have. Jesus set the example for me when he asked Peter, "Shall I not drink the cup the Father has given me?" (John 18:11).

Sometimes it has been agony to accept my cup. When my sister was slowly dying and in great pain, I refused to think about it for fear that if I started crying, I'd never be able to stop and would shatter into pieces. I was afraid that the tremendous pain and sorrow in losing her would destroy me. And then God used the title of a book to get my attention: *Don't Waste Your Sorrows.* I realized I was refusing to embrace the sorrows God had assigned to me and, in refusing, to learn from them. That day I said, "All right, Lord. I'm going to sit here and think and cry and grieve. You've given me what's in this cup. Don't let me waste it."

Sadness was overwhelming for a time, but as I wept and cried out to the Lord, my sorrow was infused with God's peace and comfort. I didn't become a basket case, as I'd feared. Instead, God restored and refreshed my spirit.

One couple told us of their horror and devastation when their only son, the apple of their eye, was killed in a tractor accident just before he was to head off to one of the military academies. We talked with them a year later, and their marriage was struggling. But it wasn't the death of their son that was destroying their marriage; it was the husband's refusal to talk about it, or to comfort and be comforted.

While his wife was talking to us, he sat stoically, his arms crossed in front of him, leaning slightly away from her and us. His demeanor shouted, "I will not be a part of this!" While denying his grief, he was emotionally unreachable, and his wife felt abandoned and alone. That man was refusing to accept his cup of sorrows, and in doing so, was blocking the life-giving water of the Lord's restorative joy as well.

There may be a few people in this world who surrender everything, including their portion and cup, and never look back. But most of us surrender in bits and pieces. Even though we may say, "Anywhere, anytime, anything, Lord," we hold back when the "anything" comes.

My friend, what is it that *you* haven't yet surrendered? Are you resenting your portion? Or are you angry about the cup God has asked you to accept? If so, your joy is being dampened, perhaps even drowned.

In order to obey God, you must surrender to His will. Part of surrendering to His will is accepting that will—a part of which is receiving both your portion and your cup. So take a good long look at your portion—your background, personality, family, appearance, gifts, talents—and surrender it all to the Lord who gave it to you. Then consider your cup—the sorrows and joys of your life—and tell Him you want to receive that cup fully—even welcome it—and learn from what it holds.

Nobody has said that acceptance, surrender, or obedience is easy. But I'm discovering that when I look at my life head-on and say to the Father, "All right, Sovereign Lord, I'm going to welcome enthusiastically not only the good things but the difficult ones; I'm going to obey You with my whole heart; I'm going to surrender all my days and moments to Your will," then joy is the flag that is flung high from the castle of my heart.

"For I know the plans I have for you," declares the LORD,
"plans to prosper you and not to harm you,
plans to give you hope and a future."

JEREMIAH 29:11

# Chapter 28

# WHOM DO YOU SERVE?

*Obedient*

Jack collapsed in his favorite chair in the family room, discouragement written all over his face. He sighed wearily and said, "Today I realized why I've been struggling and frustrated in this job. I analyzed what I'm doing and discovered that 80 percent of my job description is outside the range of my God-given gifts. I can do the job okay, but there's little joy in it. I'm thinking of turning in my resignation."

And the next day he did just that.

The following night, however, Jack couldn't sleep and spent most of the night praying and reading Scripture. The next morning he told me, "I've got to tell my boss that I was wrong. I have no peace at all, and I should not have resigned."

Amazingly, in the following weeks, Jack's attitude did a turnaround. The job didn't change, but Jack found joy in serving apart from his gifts because he realized he was being obedient to God by serving Him in this particular position.

There's a school of thought that says Christians should explore the nature of their spiritual gifts in order to determine where they should consider serving, and that we're at our most effective (with the least amount of effort and frustration) when we're serving in our areas of giftedness. There's a lot of truth in this, but it has a subtle and dangerous spin to it. While God has given each of us a unique gift in order to help serve the body of Christ in a special way, if we decide "that's the only way I'm going to serve," then we're in danger of limiting how God might choose to use us for His purposes.

At times God has asked me to serve Him in an area outside my giftedness—or at least what I think might be my gifts. It is precisely at this point that God says, "Are you willing to serve in whatever area I ask?" When I do, I have to lean completely on Him; I'm more aware than ever of my absolute dependence.

I don't have the gift of administration, but I've had to organize and direct a few women's conferences in my life. You can believe I sought help from those who had the gifts I lacked! But directing those conferences stretched me because I had to trust God in new ways for every small detail.

I'm not a great cook (would that be a result of the gift of helps?), but I've had to cook for a couple of weekend conferences for over 150 people. I remember working nearly all night—both nights—to do it too! I collapsed when it was over.

Some serve with public gifts while others minister in quiet ways, and each has her own struggles. I identified with what Ruth Calkin wrote:

> *You know, Lord, how I serve You*
> *With great emotional fervor*
> *In the limelight.*
> *You know how eagerly I speak for You*
> *At a women's club.*
> *You know how I effervesce when I promote*
> *A fellowship group.*
> *You know my genuine enthusiasm*
> *At a Bible study.*

*But how would I react, I wonder*
*If You pointed to a basin of water*
*And asked me to wash the callused feet*
*Of a bent and wrinkled old woman*
*Day after day*
*Month after month*
*In a room where nobody saw*
*And nobody knew.*[1]

I enjoy speaking at a women's group after all the hard work has been done—the planning, decorating, and "thinking through" on a hundred and one things. But some people die inside if they have to stand in front of a group. Their preference is to serve in the background.

Ruth is one of the dearest people I know. She was an effective leader of a small-group Bible study and the women in her group loved her dearly. But when we asked her to share her testimony in a larger outreach gathering, she immediately declined.

We urged her to reconsider and pray about it. A week later, she called me and said, "I'm scared to death, but I feel the Lord would have me do it." For the next month, she prayed and prepared, and it was an awful time for her. She couldn't eat, sleep, or concentrate on anything but speaking, and when she got up to give her talk, she was terrified.

But of course, everyone she knew was praying for her! Her testimony touched the hearts of many who were listening. As a result, she kept being asked to share publicly. Each time she died a thousand deaths inside, but the Lord used Ruth several times to reach women in this way. However, Ruth never volunteered!

Why did she do something she didn't enjoy? Because God asked her to. What other reason do we need?

When we're asked to do something that is out of our comfort zone, we should not immediately refuse. Instead we should pray about the opportunity, asking God if this is something He wants us to do. You might hear Him whisper, "Child of my heart, do it. Trust Me to do it through you. And remember, you're doing it for Me!"

Work from the heart for your real Master, for God,
confident that you'll get paid in full when you come
into your inheritance. Keep in mind always that the ultimate
Master you're serving is Christ.

COLOSSIANS 3:23-24, MSG

# Chapter 29

# THE GOD WHO SEES YOU

*Obedient*

Her tears made small rivulets in the dusty ground as she lay in the sand and wept. *I'm going to die,* Hagar thought, *and no one will even care.*

Her thoughts drifted back over the past few months. She remembered her humiliation when Abraham bought her as a slave. She had become a nobody with no rights, no say, no life.

Although they were old, God had promised Abraham and his wife, Sarah, a son. When the years passed and it didn't happen, Sarah had taken matters into her own hands. "Abraham," she'd demanded, "go sleep with my slave Hagar, and perhaps she'll have a baby for me." Abraham complied and Hagar became pregnant.

But there was no joy in Mudville! Sarah decided that Hagar was "looking down at her," and Sarah had taken her complaints to Abraham, blaming him for the whole miserable mess. "Do whatever you want with her," Abraham told his wife.

Hagar shuddered as she remembered the cruel physical and verbal abuse that Sarah had heaped on her. Eventually she felt that her only option was to run away, even though she had nowhere to run and could die in the wilderness. She ran as far as her strength would carry her, then collapsed in the dirt beside a spring of water, sobbing. She thought, *I'm pregnant. Alone. Nobody knows where I am. And nobody cares either.*

She couldn't have been more wrong. God knew exactly where she was and sent the "angel of the Lord" (really the Lord Himself as we find out in Genesis 16) to speak to her. God could have addressed Hagar by saying, "Hey, you there in the desert" or "Dejected one" or "Egyptian slave." Instead, He called her by name: "Hagar, servant of Sarah." It was as though He said, "I know where you are, Hagar, and I know *who* you are. I know you intimately, and I am here for you."

God asked Hagar two questions: "Where have you come from, and where are you going?" She answered only the first. (She had no clue how to answer the second.) "I'm running away from my mistress, Sarah." Then God told her something she certainly didn't want to hear: "Go back to your mistress and submit to her."

Return and submit?

Ouch!

But then, because our God is such a gracious Father, He added both encouragement and a promise. He promised Hagar that she'd have a son, and encouraged her by saying she should name him Ishmael, which means "God hears." God's words brought wonder and joy to Hagar's heart, causing her to exclaim, "You are the God who sees me" (v. 13).

Later on, when Ishmael was a child, Hagar and her son were sent from their home, and once more she thought both she and her son would die. But again God came to provide for her and give her direction and a promise. This time God said, "Leave, and I'll take care of you" (Genesis 21:8-20).

Hagar blesses my heart! God came to her in her distress two different times, and she obeyed both times, even though she must have been afraid. She chose to surrender her will, accept God's plan, and embrace the results of that plan.

My friend, stop a minute right here. Are you in a difficult situation from which you'd like to flee? (Perhaps you already have.) Take a few moments to bring your impossible circumstances to the "God who sees you," and then listen to Him. He may say, "Return and submit. I've got you just where you need to be for me to work in your life and hone your character to be more like My Son's." Or He may say, "Go ahead and leave, and I'll take care of you."

But let it be His choice, not yours.

> If you obey my commands, you will remain in my love,
> just as I have obeyed my Father's commands
> and remain in his love.
>
> JOHN 15:10

Chapter 30

# SAYING YES
# TO GOD

*Obedient*

Jack and I had first met James and Barbara when we shared a meal in their modest home in Nigeria in the late 1980s. We were delighted to see the ministry they were having in that country, but a few years later one terror-filled night changed their whole world forever.

Only half his face remained. The other half was destroyed when a bullet sliced through his head, demolished an ear, destroyed an eye, crushed part of his brain, and left him lying in a pool of his own blood. He didn't hear the cries of his wife as the attackers raped her. Nor was he aware of the marauders' ripping his house apart, sparing only his children. He was flown from Nigeria to his home in England and remained unconscious for nine days as doctors fought to save his life.

Two years later, James and Barbara shared the events of that night with a small group in Colorado Springs. As I looked at James I had to blink back tears. Where once his quick grin created crinkles around the edges of his eyes, now only one side of his face moved, twisting his countenance into a grimace. Where once his face mirrored his feelings of love, concern, goodwill, and sorrow, now expressions were limited to one eye and a few muscles around his mouth.

But I stood in awe and wonder as I listened to James's sometimes halting words and Barbara's soft ones. There was no bitterness. Only acceptance. No hatred, only love. No resentment, only forgiveness.

And their ministry had thrived. People who had never listened before, listened now. How could they not as they looked into those contorted features and heard James speak of relinquishment, acceptance, forgiveness, love.

James and Barbara took everything they had and were and placed it in the hands of God. Years before that fateful night they had surrendered their lives, time, service, and material goods. Now they had walked a huge step further—surrendering health, appearance, and even the ability to smile or to see a beloved one smile.

God spoke deeply to my heart that day as I realized how much I still have to learn about surrender and obedience.

When the angel told Mary, the mother of Jesus, that she was to give birth without being married, she replied, "I am the Lord's servant, and I am willing to accept whatever he wants" (Luke 1:38, NLT). She didn't say, "I am willing to do what You want," but "I am willing to *accept* what You want."

Think for a moment about that amazing scene of the young Jewish girl who had never been with a man. I picture her in a small courtyard on an ordinary day, listening to donkeys braying in a neighboring courtyard and hearing sandals slapping on the cobblestones outside the wall. Suddenly an angel appears, telling her not only that she's going to have a child, but that the child will be the Son of God!

Mary's face naturally expresses shock, amazement, confusion, wonder. What the angel is saying doesn't make sense. However, I imagine her bowing her head and heart as she whispers a sentence that will change the world: "I am the Lord's servant, and I am willing to accept whatever he wants."

Her words challenge me in every area of my life. Am I—are you—willing to accept *whatever? Whomever? Whenever?* Even to the point of having half your face blown away?

Obedience means saying *yes* to God—yes in the small decisions and sacrifices, and yes also in the big choices that cost us something. As we yield our wills to God we learn to say, "Father, God, I really do surrender...*all*."

Then he said to them all: "If anyone would come after me, he must deny himself and take up his cross daily and follow me.... What good is it for a man to gain the whole world, and yet lose or forfeit his very self?

LUKE 9:23,25

# TO REMIND YOU AGAIN...
*Obedience*

Nate Saint was one of five missionaries who were killed by the Auca Indians. He once wrote that his life did not change until he came to grips with the idea that "obedience is not a momentary option...it is a die-cast decision made beforehand." Someone else has said that selected obedience is not obedience at all, it is merely convenience.

To me, surrendering my will to the will of the Father is synonymous with obedience. Before you do this study, ask God to show you any areas in which you may be holding back in obeying—in surrendering—to your Lord.

1. How would you define *surrender?*

2. What was David's advice to his son Solomon concerning serving (surrendering to) the Lord? (See 1 Chronicles 28:9.)

3. What did Moses tell the children of Israel concerning the Lord in Deuteronomy 6:5-7?

4. What were the commands of Christ concerning His disciples' obedience?

Luke 9:23-25

Matthew 10:37-39

5. Who is the ultimate example of what it means to surrender to God? Write out these verses in your own words:

Hebrews 10:7,9

John 4:34

Ephesians 5:2

6. What does Christ say in Matthew 12:50 about those who do His will?

7. According to Psalm 40:8, what will help us in doing God's will?

8. According to 1 John 2:17 and 1 Peter 2:5, what will be the result of surrendering your will to God?

9. What is one area of your life in which you have the most difficulty surrendering to God? Why do you think this is? What do you think God would have you do about it?

# Chapter 31

# Costly Compassion

*Forgiving*

I studied the couple across the long wooden table in the conference center dining room as they told us their story. His large hand held her small one beneath the table, and his rugged face softened when his frequent glances brushed her face. They took turns telling us about their rocky past.

The rules were strict in the sheriff's department where Buck was a police officer, so when he began an affair, he hid it well from everyone—everyone that is, except his wife, Emily. He seemed to take sadistic pleasure in telling her when he was going to see or spend the night with his mistress. But while Emily had biblical grounds for divorce, she never wavered in her commitment to Buck or to their marriage. She told him, "I love you enough for both of us, and I'll always love you." This only made him more flagrant, more derisive, more cruel. His small daughter withdrew. His teenage son hated him. His wife, unsure what to do, prayed. And each time she considered leaving, God clearly directed her to stay.

After nearly three years Buck's mistress caused a scene in a bar, exposing not only the affair but some other shady offenses as well. Buck not only lost his job, but also his freedom. His son told him that if, after prison, his father ever moved back home, he would move out. His daughter withdrew further into her own world. Only Emily continued to tell him, "I love you and will always love you."

At last the high, hard walls Buck had built around his soul shattered. A broken man, he asked God for forgiveness and, with shame and tears, begged his wife and family to forgive him as well. It didn't take long for his daughter to blossom again, but it took some time before his son could once more live with the family. Emily's compassion and commitment never wavered, and she continued to tell her husband, "I love you, and I'll always love you."

As I listened to their story, I thought, *It's no wonder he adores you. Most wives would have left long ago.* I've known other godly women whom God has called to separate until their husbands repented and changed their ways. But God led Emily to stay with Buck, and then He gave her the capacity to keep on loving and forgiving him, even when he didn't change.

I've only personally seen such compassion and forgiveness a few times in my life. A drunk driver killed Doug's daughter and son-in-law in a car accident. His grandson was permanently disabled. Doug went to see the driver in prison to tell him that both Doug and the family had forgiven him, and Doug had the privilege of leading that man to Christ.

Jerry and Mary's lives were torn apart when a man shot and killed their only son as he was driving a taxi, but they found it in their hearts to forgive the killer even though he never asked.

Recently, as Myra stood on a curbed median waiting to cross the street, she was killed instantly by a drunk driver who'd been celebrating her birthday all afternoon. Friends of Myra's not only prayed for the woman, but contacted her in jail, assuring her of God's love and their forgiveness. She, too, has received Christ as her personal Savior.

As I listened to Emily that afternoon, I marveled at the extent of her marital commitment, her compassion, and her forgiveness—all exemplified by Christ as He interacted with lost people. Both Emily and Christ extended forgiveness to people who didn't deserve it. Both cared when that care wasn't returned. Both loved the unlovely. Both were unwavering in their commitment.

The Lord went far beyond that, of course. He who was absolutely pure and clean became defiled and filthy for those who had no comprehension or appreciation of what He was doing. He was tortured, spit upon, ridiculed, and then died a horrible death to take upon Himself what I deserved: judgment, punishment, and separation from the Father.

Even now as I think about Emily, I hear her words to her husband, "I love you and I'll always love you." And as I think about Christ, I hear Him saying, "Child, I love you. *I'll always love you.*" And my heart fills with praise.

Be kind and compassionate to one another,
forgiving each other, just as in Christ God forgave you.

EPHESIANS 4:32

# Chapter 32

# FORGIVENESS IS NOT A FEELING

*Forgiving*

"Will my mother be in heaven?" this abused-as-a-child woman asked. And then, before I could say anything, she added, "Because if she's going to be in heaven, I don't want to go there."

Everyone I know has wrestled with forgiveness—for big things as well as small, for everyday offenses as well as once-in-a-lifetime events. Our decision about whether to forgive affects our spiritual peace, emotional health, physical well-being, and personal joy.

David Augsburger writes this about forgiveness:

Forgiveness is hard. Especially in a [relationship] tense with past troubles, tormented by fears of rejection and humiliation, and torn by suspicion and distrust.

Forgiveness hurts. Especially when it must be extended to a [person] who doesn't deserve it, who hasn't earned it, who may misuse it. It hurts to forgive.

Forgiveness costs. Especially in a [relationship] when it means accepting instead of demanding repayment for the wrong done; where it means releasing the other instead of exacting revenge; where it means reaching out in love instead of relishing resentments. It costs to forgive.[1]

Yet all of us know who pays the greatest price when we don't forgive. We do. Someone has said "Bitterness hurts the vessel it's stored in more than the one it is poured out upon." It's true.

In *Married Lovers, Married Friends,* Steve and Annie Chapman write of one woman who'd been violently molested who said,

"Whenever I thought about forgiving this person who violated me so cruelly, I could not let that hurt go because he deserved to pay. The truth is, my thoughts of hatred and bitterness had absolutely no effect on him, but they were tearing my life apart...."

This woman suffered crippling arthritis, broken relationships, and immense depression, which didn't begin to change until she decided that, with God's help, she would begin actively to forgive her offender. She said, "If I had a thought of hatred for this man—and I had many—I'd acknowledge the thought (not deny it), and then I would thank the Lord for how it would drive me to God. Then I would concentrate on God's love, and His ability to forgive me no matter what I had done. I especially worked on thinking of Scripture passages that helped me focus on God's truth—like 1 John 4:7 that says, 'Dear friend, let us love one another, for love comes from God.' It helped me to choose to forgive this man.

"After all this I would pray for his salvation, and then ask God to give me divine forgiveness from my heart. It seemed I had to go through the same process a hundred times a day for a while. But after I relinquished my hatred, God did a real healing in my life."[2]

One of my friends struggles with anger toward her son-in-law. The truth is, he is a no-good, immature, uncouth, dysfunctional man who has a trigger temper and frequently walks away from his family, responsibilities, and job. He seems to have no insight into how he's hurting his family. When I asked this friend to name the thing she has to learn over and over, she said, "forgiveness." When she sees her precious grandchildren being hurt, when she finds her daughter in tears, when she is personally and verbally attacked by this man, she can almost taste the resentment and bitterness, like bile rising in her throat And just when she has prayed and worked through forgiving one more time, this man does something else.

When I see my friend's pain and hear such stories, I, too, can get angry and even bitter—even though the offense is not against me. But like her, I must forgive and put the matter into my Father's hands. My friend told me that many times she simply has to will herself to forgive her son-in-law. She has to forgive him in faith and not in feeling because sometimes the feeling of forgiveness doesn't come until long after she has made the *decision* to forgive.

Jane took a different route. She grew up feeling her mother hated her. Even as an adult, when Jane went home (as infrequently as possible!), her mother either ignored her or said cruel things to her. Whenever she called, her mom cut her down and left her in tears. Jane grew to hate her mom for hating *her* and for the feelings of inadequacy and inferiority that resulted from her mom's actions and words.

But Jane loved God and knew that He wanted her to forgive her mother. Sounded easy. Wasn't. One day Jane meditated on Colossians 3:13, "Forgive whatever grievances you may have against one another. Forgive as the Lord forgave you." That week, Jane listed everything she could think of that her mom had done which caused her pain. It took an entire morning and she cried all the way through it. Then she wrote out another list: the sins she had committed against God, beginning with, "I hate my mother." She cried all the way through that list, too.

Then Jane took a red pen and wrote across her list of sins: FOR-GIVEN THROUGH THE BLOOD OF CHRIST. Next, very slowly and deliberately, she took that red pen and wrote across the list of the things her mother had done: I FORGIVE YOU AS GOD HAS FOR-GIVEN ME.

Jane did one final thing. She took both lists out into the back yard, dug a hole, and buried them. With this act, Jane consciously forgave her mother.

How was she able to do this? She *chose* to forgive—she didn't wait until she *felt* like forgiving.

This is one of the most important—and difficult—lessons I've learned about forgiveness: My will must control my emotions (which pull the opposite way quite often!). Resentment and unforgiveness are not viable choices for children of God. God *commands* me to forgive.

Difficult? Yes.

Impossible? Sometimes it seems so.

Until I remember that nothing is impossible with God.

I can do everything through him who gives me strength.

PHILIPPIANS 4:13

# Chapter 33

# "Jump; I'll Catch You!"

*Forgiving*

It was a lively exchange between another couple and Jack and me. Bob was upset because he hadn't been treated fairly or justly. He was deeply hurt and frustrated because there wasn't a thing he could do about an injustice he had experienced. Both he and his wife commented, "It just isn't right!"

And it wasn't.

But then Bob made a comment that struck my heart. He said he'd recently had lunch with a man who was a lot like him. This man was dealing with depression and anger and had consulted a godly counselor for help. The insight he received was this: Some people, like him and Bob, are wired to want to make things *right*. And when they are able to rectify a situation, they temporarily feel satisfied. But it's only temporary. Soon something else comes along that isn't just, and they feel a desperate need to correct it. If they can't, they're frustrated; if they can, they have another temporary feeling of satisfaction—until something else comes along that needs to be fixed.

The counselor said, "But there is another way to deal with situations that aren't just or right. *Grace*. When you extend grace instead of demanding justice, rather than getting temporary satisfaction you benefit for eternity."

138

Think about it. First Corinthians 6:7-8 says, "Why not just accept the injustice and leave it at that? Why not let yourselves be cheated? But instead, you yourselves are the ones who do wrong" (NLT).

Dianne Hales writes, "To forgive doesn't mean to give in; it means to let go…. A rabbi who lost his family in the Holocaust told us he forgave because he chose not to bring Hitler with him to America. When you forgive, you reclaim your power to choose. It doesn't matter whether someone deserves forgiveness; *you* deserve to be free."[1]

Sometimes I feel so helpless in this matter of forgiving. If I had to do it all by myself, it would be impossible. But I don't have to do it myself. God will help me as I ask Him for *His* grace.

One of my favorite authors, Ron Mehl, wrote:

I remember hearing about a terrible house fire that swept through the home of a young couple with four children. Mom and Dad got the little ones out safely, but one of their boys suddenly bolted back into the blazing house and dashed up the stairs to look for his pet. In just seconds flames turned that stairwell into a roaring inferno, and no one could run after him. Somehow the little boy found his way to an upstairs window, and the father yelled, "Son, jump! I can catch you! *Jump now!*"

Filled with terror, the boy wailed, "But Daddy, I can't see you!"

His father immediately replied, "Son, it doesn't matter. I can see *you!*"

Trusting his dad's voice, the little boy jumped blindly into the smoke…and into his father's arms.

Stalled in a dead end of hesitation and doubt, you may find yourself saying, "Lord, I can't see You. I'm in the middle of all this hurt and confusion, and I can't see Your hand in any of this. I can't see Your love and care."[2]

When we have been deliberately wronged, and the hurt is so great it's tearing us apart, in our own strength it's impossible to forgive, to let go and "jump." But it's in those times—and they'll come to every one of us—we'll hear the Lord saying, "Jump! I'll catch you! My grace is sufficient for you."

And so we jump. And suddenly we find we've escaped the fire of bitterness. We're free, safe in His grace-full arms.

He shielded him and cared for him;
he guarded him as the apple of his eye,
like an eagle that stirs up its nest and hovers over its young,
that spreads its wings to catch them
and carries them on its pinions.

DEUTERONOMY 32:10-11

# TO REMIND YOU AGAIN...
## *Forgiveness*

A wise counselor was asked, "How do you forgive someone?" Leaning over the coffee shop table, he wrote on a place mat:

The mind analyzes.

The emotions react.

The will chooses.

Then he added, "Don't let your emotions tell you what to do."

We *choose* to forgive.

But it's not easy.

1. What does God's Word have to say about forgiveness in the following verses?

Psalm 86:5

Psalm 103:3-4

2. What is the biblical basis for our forgiveness?

Ephesians 1:7-8

Colossians 1:13-14

3. God's forgiveness of our sin carries a condition. What is it?

1 John 1:9

4. What are the reasons we should forgive those who have hurt us?

Matthew 6:12-15

Matthew 18:21-22

Mark 11:25

Colossians 3:13

5. Is there a person you are struggling to forgive at this moment? What would God have you do, and why?

6. What are the steps you are willing to take to forgive? When? Will you allow yourself to be accountable to a friend in this matter?

7. Memorize at least one verse concerning forgiveness and keep a list of others to memorize in the future.

# Chapter 34

# "YEA, GOD!"

## *Worshipful*

The gondola swayed and creaked as it moved ponderously up Vail mountain on this bright day, as untarnished as a newly minted penny. When the gondola completed its journey halfway up the mountain, Jack and I and our daughter, Lynn, her husband, Tim, and their children, Eric and Sunny, clambered out into the sunshine. Then the six of us started up the hiking trail in order to have a family picnic on a wooden platform high above the ski bowls.

Suddenly a huge eagle swooped over the trail fifty feet ahead of us. We gasped, laughing in sheer delight at God's creation and the blessing of being together on this outing.

And then Tim raised his arms to the sky and shouted at the top of his lungs, "YEA, GOD!"

It was a moment of pure and enthusiastic worship.

Growing up, I thought worship only happened in church. To me, it meant a solemn prayer or a majestic hymn or the beauty of stained-glass windows. How wrong I was! Worship should be something that happens in my heart all day, every day. But some days I am so self-absorbed that I fail to be absorbed by God's majesty. Some days my worship comes in snatches…but I do long for it to be *one continual act.*

Thinking about this one day, I wrote:

*Lord, I want my life—*
   *my whole life, my everyday life—to be*
      *one work*
      *of worship*
      *for You.*
*Whatever I'm doing today,*
   *may it be worship.*
*When I'm involved in the dailies,*
   *may it be worship.*
*When I'm catching up on office things—*
   *letters, mailing—*
   *may it be worship.*
*When I'm writing, creating,*
   *may it be worship.*
*When I'm learning the new computer program,*
   *may it be worship.*
*Whether I'm serving others,*
   *relaxing,*
   *eating,*
   *traveling,*
   *witnessing,*
   *speaking…*
*Oh, Lord,*
   *may it be worship.*

Having a heart and mind continuously absorbed in worship is my ultimate goal. But as I'm growing toward that goal, I want more times of spontaneous and exuberant worship—like Tim expressed that day on the mountain.

I also want more times of deliberate worship. I'm ashamed when I compare my lack of fervor in worshiping God to some people's in other religious traditions. I have seen men and women chanting and spinning prayer wheels over and over and over; old women laboring up long staircases on their knees; men whipping themselves to do penance for their sins; others prostrating themselves in prayer in the hot sun. And I ask myself, when was the last time I prostrated myself before God?

Of course, I could argue that these people are trying to earn their way to heaven and my salvation isn't dependent on my works, but on Christ's redemptive work on the cross. Yet shouldn't my gratefulness for my salvation be as fervent as their working for theirs?

Initially my salvation did cause me to worship more spontaneously and constantly. When I knelt with my mother beside my bed when I was twelve and asked Jesus to come into my life and be my Savior and Lord, my heart was filled with joy and thanksgiving…and *worship*. I know that the wonder of my salvation should *continue* to fill my heart with worship. And yet too often I find myself—when I think about it at all—having a complacent attitude, a sort of "Well, yeah, I'm glad I'm saved. So let's get on with the 'what else.'"

That should not be! For unless my heart quickens with joy when I think of my salvation, the "what else" may not inspire me to worship either.

*Oh Father, thank You that my future is secure. Infuse my heart with fresh wonder at Your splendor and righteousness. I want to feel like shouting with my son-in-law: "YEA, GOD!"*

Every day.

All the time.

> They rejoice in your name all day long;
> they exult in your righteousness.
> For you are their glory and strength.
>
> PSALM 89:16-17

# Chapter 35

# HUMBLE
# ADORATION

*Worshipful*

In his book *Heaven Help Us!* Steven Lawson tells a story about a man who was walking through an art gallery when he came upon a picture of Jesus Christ dying on the cross. He stopped and looked at the beautiful portrait of Calvary's love.

As he stared into the face of Christ, so full of agony, the gallery guard tapped him on the shoulder. "Lower," the guard said. "The artist painted this picture to be appreciated from a lower position."

So the man bent down. And from this lower position, he observed new beauties in the picture he'd previously not seen.

Then the guard interrupted him again. "Lower," he said. "Lower still."

The man knelt on one knee and looked up into the face of Christ. The new vantage point yielded additional treasures to behold and appreciate.

But motioning with his flashlight toward the ground, the attendant said, "Lower. You've got to go lower."

Only as the man dropped onto both knees and looked up could he realize the artist's intended perspective. Only then could he see the full beauty of the Cross.[1]

God touched my heart as I pondered the significance of this story and realized how it describes true worship.

The Greek word for *worship* means "to kiss toward, to kiss the hand, to bow down." It means to "bow before a sovereign ruler in humble adoration. It means to ascribe 'worth-ship' to something or someone. Thus worship is recognizing and responding to who God is and affirming His supreme value. When we talk about worship, we are talking about something we give to God. It is an all-consuming, selfless desire to give to God our lives, our praise, our possessions, our attitudes, our all."[2]

That's what the inner attitude of worship is—a demeanor that says, "I'm not worthy to come before You, Father, and I'm overwhelmed and grateful that You allow me to come so boldly into Your presence."

What comes to your mind as you picture someone worshiping? I think of someone with eyes closed, kneeling or bowing, or even prostrating himself before the object of his worship—and actually, that's scriptural. Psalm 95:6-7 says: "Come, let us bow down in worship, let us kneel before the LORD our Maker; for he is our God and we are the people of his pasture, the flock under his care." All through the Old Testament we find people kneeling to worship. Second Chronicles 29:29 says, "When the offerings were finished, the king and everyone present with him knelt down and worshiped." An attitude of humility is demonstrated by kneeling, and God is pleased with a humble heart. Isaiah 66:2 proclaims, "This is the one I esteem: he who is humble and contrite in spirit, and trembles at my word."

When I began to study about worship, words concerning humility seemed to leap from the page and imbed themselves in my heart— verses such as: "Since the first day that you set your mind to gain understanding and to humble yourself before your God, your words were heard..." (Daniel 10:12). The prophet Zephaniah (2:3) said, "Seek the LORD, all you humble of the land, you who do what he commands. Seek righteousness, seek humility."

Actually, God's Word *commands* me to be humble—to "lower myself." Do you ever have conversations with yourself? I do. I not only ask myself questions and answer back, but sometimes I even argue with myself! That's what happened when I read 1 Peter 5:6, which says, "Humble yourselves, therefore, under God's mighty hand, that he may lift you up in due time."

My heart asked, "But how do I humble *myself*? I know God humbles me, especially when I ask. (I admit I don't ask very often— it's too humbling!) But how do I humble *myself* under His mighty hand?"

My mind chewed on that awhile and then responded, "In a very practical way, I humble myself as I choose to deliberately take the 'lower' position with members of the family of God." I remembered a description of dying to self I'd read recently: "When your good is evil spoken of, when your wishes are crossed, your advice disregarded, your opinions ridiculed, and you refuse to let anger rise in your heart, or even defend yourself, but take it all in patient, loving silence—that is DYING TO SELF."

I almost choked on that one! And yet I had to consider the phrases "you refuse to let anger rise in your heart…you refuse to defend yourself…"—two actions I can deliberately take to humble myself. By humbling myself with God's servants, I learn the heart attitude I need to worship God.

My heart confessed, "I'm not very good at this, Lord." A light came on in my mind. I thought of refusing to play the bragging or name-dropping game, eradicating as many "I" and "me" words from my vocabulary as possible, and deliberately turning conversations to the other person instead of going on and on about myself. With these actions I lower myself, humble myself, die to self.

Humility and worship go hand in hand. While humility in outward worship is often demonstrated by bowing or kneeling, inward worship is the *continual* bowing of my heart before God.

My heart was wide-eyed as I asked, "But how do I worship *continually?*"

My mind struggled on that one, then haltingly responded, "I think one of the keys is preparation. Just as the set-aside times of worship take advanced thought and planning, so the ongoing worship of a person's heart takes even more."

I sighed as my heart questioned, "So how do I *do* that?"

It was then the Father brought to mind the various ways I've observed people preparing for—and actually—worshiping. One godly man I heard speak says that the first thing he does when he gets up in the morning is to kneel beside his bed and praise God for who He is. Another recites chapters of the Bible he's memorized as he walks to and from work. I realized that part of my own preparation was taking a few minutes each morning to commune with God—to sit at His feet and listen in a concentrated way—which helps me to be more attuned to His whispers throughout the rest of the day. Warren and Ruth Myers write: "We...need to see God as the Creator and Sustainer of all things, majestic and holy and awesome—a sovereign God, exalted far above all, the Source of all that we humans take pride in."[3] When I sit at His feet, I'm bowing before His majesty and focusing my heart on the One who is All in All.

Finally, after much reflection, my heart said, "Father, I'm beginning to realize that it is essential to *choose* to continually fill my mind with who You are. I'm starting to understand that it's critical to *strive* to be humble and lowly before You. But oh, how I need Your help! I long for You, Father. I want my heart to be constantly bowing before You in wonderful, beautiful, awesome, and glorious worship."

And the Father said, "Beloved, keep listening and keep learn-ing...*because I want that too!*"

You are worthy, our Lord and God,
to receive glory and honor and power,
for you created all things, and by your will they were created
and have their being.

REVELATION 4:11

# Chapter 36

# Is Your Container Ready?

*Worshipful*

In those sun-warmed January days in the Southern California desert, we soon got the hang of the system. Golfers were to stick a bucket under the nozzle of the golf-ball machine, call the pro shop to give their name, and then some invisible person would release about fifty balls into the waiting receptacle. Different than anything we'd seen, but hey, no problem.

One morning Jack casually called the pro shop to request a bucket of balls, heard the invisible clerk push the release button, and suddenly realized he had failed to put an empty bucket under the nozzle! Balls rolled everywhere, scattering on the cement below the machine, the surrounding grass, and even on the driving range. People stared and snickered as, embarrassed, we scrambled to retrieve the rolling rascals. Then one kind gentleman said, "Don't worry about it. We've all done that at least once."

I reflected on that incident as I read Colossians 1:5, which contains the phrase "hope that is *stored* up for you in heaven" (emphasis mine). I wonder... Have I sometimes missed what God wants to give me because I've called upon Him without getting my "container" ready to receive the gifts He dispenses?

For example, is my heart ready to receive more of God each time I read Scripture? God often uses His Word to fill my heart to overflowing with worship, yet there are certain sections that bog me down. Like Leviticus. Yet this morning a chapter from that very book caused me to exclaim, "What a God You are!" I was reading about how Aaron, Moses' brother, had been with and spoken for Moses. He had stood at Moses' side and had seen God's power demonstrated through the plagues in Egypt. He'd walked at the head of the throng through the Red Sea and seen the bodies of the Egyptians littered on the shore as God delivered the Israelites from their enemies. Aaron saw mighty God at work, up close and personal.

Yet when Moses was up on the mountain meeting with God longer than anyone thought he'd be, the people grew concerned and restless…and Aaron did the unthinkable.[1] He deliberately disobeyed God's commands. He asked all the people to bring him gold, and then he made them a golden calf to worship instead of God. On top of that, he lied to Moses, saying he'd thrown the gold into a fire and the calf had miraculously emerged! It's a wonder God didn't strike Aaron dead on the spot.

But later in Leviticus 8—and this is what brought me to worship—God commanded Moses to have Aaron designated the leader of His *holy* priests! So Moses placed on Aaron the sacred robe and set the royal turban on his head.

Now I can understand God being pleased with Moses. Over and over, Scripture says that Moses did "just as the Lord commanded." But Aaron?

Because my heart was listening this morning as I read this familiar story once again, God showed me afresh a bit more of His amazing mercy. But I wonder how often I read God's Word with an unprepared heart—a container not ready to receive the glorious truths God wants to pour into me.

When I pray for others, is my container ready for God's answers? We were shocked a couple of months ago when we received the news: John and Helen were out hunting, and he'd gotten out of the van to open a gate for her to drive through. Somehow she hit the accelerator instead of the brake and the vehicle ran over him, causing extensive injuries. It took Helen two hours to get John back to the ranch house of friends and another hour to get him by Flight-for-Life to the hospital.

This week John wrote:

On my last trip to the doctor he removed the cast from my right arm. My wrist had been broken in the accident and it needed surgery, as did my right arm and right foot. Soon I'll return to the doctor and he'll remove the cast from my right leg.

At the last visit, we were thrilled to learn that surgery would not be needed on my left shoulder. It had been a concern to us, since the bone in the left arm had been severed completely. The three ribs that were fractured are mending, but still sore. I'm not driving as yet and also not wearing proper clothes.

But God is good. He has taught us so much during this time. I praise Him for every lesson. Throughout my life I've gotten by with little pain and minimum sickness. In fact, I consider that I've gotten off quite light. I was sharing with a friend lately that I wouldn't trade the experience of walking with God thorough this time for anything.

Emotionally, Helen has kept pace with my healing physically. We're both rejoicing in the Lord.

John's container was ready to receive God's lessons and blessings, and my heart responded. As I read John's words, I thanked God for His grace, and I worshiped.

In the second book of Samuel we read, "[They] were celebrating with all their might" and "David...danced before the LORD with all his might" (2 Samuel 6:5,14). I long to worship like this, with all my might. God is teaching me that heartfelt worship is a lifestyle, a continuous response to God all day long. And whether it be golf balls dropped into a bucket or God's heavenly gifts dropped into my heart—may my container be ready!

> Turn my eyes away from worthless things;
> preserve my life according to your word.
>
> PSALM 119:37

# TO REMIND YOU AGAIN...
## *Worship*

Anne Ortlund tells this story:

"What does it take," someone asked a circus tightrope walker, "to do what you do?"

"Three things," he answered.

"*Raw courage*. You commit yourself to begin walking, and then you can't change your mind.

"*Balance*. You can't lean too far this way or that.

"Most of all, *concentration*. You fix your eyes on that wire, and until it's all over you never shift your attention."

He paused. Then—

"*Never*," he said firmly.[2]

Learning to worship continually takes this kind of concentration. Let's see what Scripture has to say about how to cultivate a worshipful heart.

1. Read slowly David's prayer of praise and worship in 1 Chronicles 29:10-19. List some of the things David praised and worshiped God for. Then make a list of some of the things *you* can praise and worship God for as well.

2. Read Romans 12:1-3, and then write it out in your own words. What does this passage urge us to do?

3. What do the following verses say about worship?

Psalm 95:6-7

Psalm 18:3

Psalm 86:12

Psalm 86:9

Psalm 96:9

Psalm 96:4

Psalm 145:3

4. Read Ephesians 1:3-7 and list some of the reasons to praise and worship. What is God saying to your heart from this passage? What do you think He would have you do about it?

Anne Ortlund says that focusing on Jesus continually requires giving Him "frequent spaces when you momentarily quit, relax, breathe deeply, stretch your body, and say, 'Jesus, my eyes are on You. You are able. You are helping me from one moment to the next. I trust You.'"[3] We all have many "little spaces" in our days—waiting at traffic lights, pausing while the water boils, taking a moment to put on hand lotion. If with conscious effort we would use these spaces to enjoy an interlude of concentrated worship, we would feel God's lift to our spirits. I'm sure of it!

Chapter 37

# RX FOR DISCOURAGEMENT

*Hopeful*

Tears fell as I drove away, watching Jack disappear from my sight in the rearview mirror. He had followed me for thirty miles so we could meet at a small café to talk and pray together before I traveled on to a speaking engagement at a women's conference.

Now I was on my own, and I poured out my heart. "Lord, You know I DON'T WANT TO DO THIS! Everything in me wants to stay in Vail with our kids and Jack. Tim and Lynn are under such a heavy load right now; I want to help them and not leave them. I'm tired, discouraged, unmotivated, down, scared; I hate that I have to do this! I have no strength or ability to do it. If anything is going to get done this weekend in the lives of the women who are coming, You'll have to do it all."

Amazingly, God's peace settled over my heart and the tears dried on my cheeks. Still, I had no expectations as I drove into the small rustic camp. I wasn't feeling ready or spiritually "up"—would God even work? Was the effort worth it?

When I got up to speak, my doubts only increased. Women were sitting all over the floor. (How could they listen under those conditions?) As I talked, interruptions were frequent. (Did anyone even care about what I was saying?)

Yet God was in charge. He took over in spite of me—probably *because* of my helplessness. He was obviously working in women's hearts as we saw walls of resentment crumble and tears of repentance fall.

Driving home, the Lord and I had quite a conversation about hope.

"Father, I'm sorry about my attitude at the beginning of this weekend. I felt so awful, so hopeless."

The Father spoke to my heart, "Child, yours is a sure hope, whether you believe it or not. That truth never changes—only your feelings about that truth waver. You need to remember that faith and hope go hand in hand."

I recalled the verse, "Now faith is being sure of what we hope for and certain of what we do not see" (Hebrews 11:1). I was silent as I chewed on that. "Sure hope," God had said.

Finally, I asked, "What—or who—is my hope, Lord?"

God quoted His own Word to me, "Christ in you, the hope of glory" (Colossians 1:27).

"How true!" I agreed. "I need Christ as my sure hope in every situation."

I could sense His smile as He said, "In all of life's events you need hope, My child. For instance, this weekend you needed hope for your discouraged heart. And meditating on the truth of My Word is the best prescription for discouragement." Instantly I recalled Psalm 43:5, which proclaims, "Why are you downcast, O my soul! Why so disturbed within me? Put your hope in God, for I will yet praise him, my Savior and my God."

"I certainly did need Your hope then, Father. Tell me more, please."

"You need special hope when you're anxious," He said.

I spent the next five minutes thinking of many times when anxieties had swarmed like hornets around my mind, and only the powerful antidote of God's Word could dissipate them. I recalled these soothing words: "Find rest, O my soul, in God alone; my hope comes from him" (Psalm 62:5).

God continued to put His thoughts in my mind: "You need My hope when you are weak. Remember My words, 'but those who hope in the LORD will renew their strength. They will soar on wings like eagles'" (Isaiah 40:31).

"I remember, Father."

"Those are just a start, child. You need My hope permeating your mind, your thoughts, your spirit...all the time, in every situation. Remember I said, 'Christ is all that matters, and he lives in all of us'" (Colossians 3:11, NLT).

*Christ is all that matters,* my heart echoed, *and He lives in all of us.*

Yes! When that truth is firmly wrapped around my heart, my soul will refuse to be downcast or disturbed or discouraged because I will be *filled* with hope. *His* hope!

> The LORD delights in those who fear him,
> who put their hope in his unfailing love.
>
> PSALM 147:11

Chapter 38

# THE REFINING PROCESS

*Hopeful*

I glanced at the obituaries, and gasped as I read that the son of a former next-door neighbor had been killed in a plane crash. On a cold December afternoon, Jack and I attended David's memorial service. I remembered him as a bright, happy child whose laugh and grin sparkled in a gray world. David had grown into a fine young man, married, and had three small children.

From where I sat in the sanctuary, the large front picture window framed a gray sky. And as though placed there by an unseen hand, a black angry-looking cloud hung in the middle of the window and remained throughout the service, a symbol of the pain in our hearts.

But then I noticed the words on the Christmas banners surrounding the window: HOPE. PEACE. JOY.

The banners reminded me of three encouraging truths... The HOPE of knowing that the dark cloud of death will one day dissipate, and bright blue sky and sunshine will appear for us all. The JOY of knowing that David was in heaven. And that Christ brings PEACE, even in sorrow.

I leaned sideways to see what was on the fourth banner. LOVE. The LOVE of God makes our hope and peace and joy real and abiding. Because Christ died and rose again, we are not in the land of the living doomed to the land of the dying. No, we are in the land of the dying destined for the Land of the Living!

One of my mentors died recently. Marion's memorial service was a sad/happy occasion. Make that happy/sad, because there was more joy than sadness. She had had Alzheimer's the last four years of her life. Toward the end, her brain shut down. It no longer told her that she needed food or water or that she needed to swallow.

But now Marion is free! She has a heavenly body to go with her perfectly restored brain and spirit. The joy is hers—and ours for her. But we are sad, too; we miss her. The pain and loss are real.

C. S. Lewis agonized over the death of his beloved wife, Joy, and was angry when someone said to him one day, "I think you're getting over it." He wrote that one doesn't "get over" death like one "gets over" the measles. No, he said, a death is more like an amputation of a leg. The stump may heal, but every morning and night, and many times in-between, one is aware that the leg is missing. That part never "gets better" until heaven.

Through my loss of David and Marion, God reminded me that He alone is my hope. Hebrews 6:19 says, "We have this hope as an anchor for the soul, firm and secure." Ours is not a pie-in-the-sky kind of hope, but a rock-solid hope that we can count on—a hope firmly embedded in eternity.

I need to gaze into the face of hope. As I do, I am reminded that hope's beautiful countenance is lined with suffering. Hope is refined through suffering. Romans 5:3 states this truth clearly: "Not only so, but we also rejoice in our sufferings, because we know that suffering produces perseverance; perseverance, character; and character, hope."

David Roper, in his book *Seeing Through,* says,

Just before that old soul J. Oswald Sanders went home to be with the Lord, he reminisced with Carolyn and me about an event that occurred early in his ministry. He had just delivered what he considered to be a masterful, compelling message and was leaving the building where he had spoken when he overheard a conversation between two elderly women.

"What did you think of Mr. Sanders's message?" one asked.

"Oh, he'll be all right," the other replied, "when he's suffered awhile."[1]

Mr. Sanders did suffer, ministering alone for many years around the world after his wife died. His suffering produced perseverance, and his perseverance produced hope, which was evident in his life.

In a sermon on Romans 5:3-10, Ray Stedman told of a man who had to have one of his legs amputated. But that radical procedure didn't arrest the course of his disease, and he ultimately died. Just a few days before his death, a minister visited him, and the dying man said something the minister never forgot: "I never would have chosen one of the trials that I've gone through, but I wouldn't have missed any of them for the world!" That godly man's statement perfectly expresses what Christian rejoicing in suffering is all about.

Some situations seem to go on forever without resolution. Some may continue until the end of our lives. Romans 5:3 tells us that hope is developed through a process. Suffering produces perseverance (or "patience" in the KJV), and patience produces character (or "experience"). The *outcome* of the process is hope.

In this late afternoon of my life, I can see that my ability to persevere has developed from experiencing various painful situations. My experience of God's faithfulness through those difficult trials has honed my character. And that character and experience make it much easier to have hope that God will *once again* do what He says. Oh, I may have moments of doubt and discouragement—moments and days and weeks and even months. But because the suffering in my life has produced more patience and because that perseverance has given me character born of experience—a track record with God—I'm able to cling to that Sure Hope that dwells within.

The next time you or I feel we have no hope, let's remember to pray, "Remind me again, Lord. I forget."

But the eyes of the LORD are on those who fear him,
on those whose hope is in his unfailing love.

PSALM 33:18

# Chapter 39

# A Certain Future

*Hopeful*

Tom's wife wasn't with him when he picked us up for what was to be a quick dinner at a mystery location they had selected.

"Where's Kae?" we asked.

"We're going to swing by the house," Tom replied.

Tom and Kae are special friends in our cul-de-sac, and we enjoy seeing them frequently. Both are gourmet cooks, and Jack and I love the great restaurants they find in town. But tonight as we walked into their home, candlelight and a lovely table greeted us. The "special place" that night was to be their dining room!

On our plates were cards with the *menue de noche* Tom had created. Printed in large letters, it read:

*la greens para pecan*
*pote de bako*
*le bouf au pepper brazier*
*bread de hote*
*café*
*la chocholat' de vanilla por Kae* (Kae makes her own chocolate
   sauce for ice cream that is out of this world!)

We all had a great laugh…a great dinner…a great visit.

Jack and I had expected to eat a good but predictable meal. The meal we ate was, well, extraordinary. Someday—*soon,* from eternity's perspective—Someone is going to come for me. He'll pick me up to take me to a mystery place. Then He'll take me to His home where a banquet table will be prepared, and all His other guests will greet me. It will be far beyond anything I've ever imagined!

This certain hope for eternal life should be at the forefront of my thoughts…but I'm prone to get my eyes and heart off that hope. When I do let my thoughts and imagination shift into high gear and dream about what heaven will be like, I get excited! Some things I know for sure, and others are simply possibilities.

I'm fairly sure, for instance, that all my memory cells will be on total recall, that I'll remember every single person I've met on this earth and all I know about each person (well, the good things anyhow). I won't have to say, "Let's see, where did I meet you?" I'll remember everything I'm told up there—forever! (Hey, won't that be great?)

I don't think everyone will be able to do everything, or we wouldn't appreciate the unique gifts and work of others. But I'm going to be able to play the piano. (I play now, but I'll be *much* better in heaven!) My fingers will be at their most dexterous, my knowledge at its highest peak. I'll be able to memorize music as I read it. I'll have to practice—but that will be a joy, given how my fingers feel and how well I play!

I think I'm going to be able to explore other planets. I'll plan adventures to do this with special people. And—this one is fun to think about—I think we're going to be able to go in and out of "time" as we know it. I'll be able to step back in time and see the earth being formed, the Red Sea parting, Lazarus being raised from the dead. I'll be able to follow Christ around during His time on earth. (Won't that be something?). When you and I are talking about some event in your life, I'll be able to say, "Let's go back and look at that." I'll be able to see events I missed in the lives of Lynn, Tim, Eric, and Sunny when they lived in Mexico for ten years. I'll be able to see and hear that God-blessed men's conference Jack was so thrilled to be a part of. I'll be able to hear my grandfather's first sermon when he pioneered a church in an old mining town in Yampa, Colorado.

Yes, I know—I could be wrong about all this. God says that eye hasn't seen nor ear heard nor has it even entered into the heart of man the things God has prepared for us. So I don't know exactly what heaven will be like. But one thing is certain: Heaven will be far better than I can imagine!

Paul wrote, "If the dead are not raised, 'Let us eat and drink for tomorrow we die'" (1 Corinthians 15:32). But, praise God, there is a heaven! There is a resurrection. Eternity stretches before us in unimaginable glory. We can be sure about that.

Oh, I'm sure of one more thing: My welcoming dinner is going to surpass even *la chocholat' de vanilla por Kae!*

Since you have been raised to new life with Christ,
set your sights on the realities of heaven....
Let heaven fill your thoughts.

COLOSSIANS 3:1-2 (NLT)

# TO REMIND YOU AGAIN...
## *Hope*

Hope. Aren't you glad for it? In a sermon on Mark 16:1-8, Ray Stedman quoted Dr. Carl F. Henry, one of America's leading contemporary theologians, who said recently of Jesus, "He planted the only durable rumor of hope amid the widespread despair of a hopeless world."

Aren't you glad He did?

1. Read carefully and prayerfully, and then paraphrase the following verses:

   Lamentations 3:21-24

   Romans 5:1-5

   Romans 15:13

2. Pray Ephesians 1:18, putting your name in it.

3. Make an outline with the following points and verses.

   In whom or what does our hope rest?

   Colossians 1:27

   Psalm 25:21; 33:22; 62:5-6

   Psalm 119:43,114; 130:5

Psalm 147:11

Romans 15:4

Titus 1:2

Titus 2:13

What results from our hope in God?

Psalm 25:3

Psalm 31:24

Psalm 42:5

Psalm 33:18

Psalm 33:20

Isaiah 40:31

1 Peter 1:3-5

1 Peter 3:15

When should we have hope?

Psalm 25:5

Psalm 71:14

Commands concerning hope:

Romans 12:12

4. Choose one verse that God put on your heart during this study, and memorize that verse.

5. Write out the verse in your own words, giving a specific recent example of how you've failed to obey this verse. Then write down three steps you feel God would have you take to put this verse into practice.

# REMIND ME AGAIN, LORD

The dusty white car pulled to a stop in our driveway, and Jack and I rushed out to greet our brother-in-law Fred with enthusiastic hugs and grins.

Fred is rarely too tired to smile, and his sly grin told us he was up to something as he said, "I've got something for you."

"Oh?" my eyebrows raised. "What is it?"

"Come look," he insisted.

We walked to the back of his car as Fred opened the trunk. On the floor in the back was a large, somewhat battered, whitewashed, dusty, and very old ox yoke. He explained, "Before Joye died, she had been looking for an ox yoke for you. She knew you wanted one, but she'd never been able to find one. Then this winter, I saw this one in an old barn, and the people agreed to sell it to me."

As soon as I could, I took it to an antique restorer and asked if he could refinish it. A week later he called. "It's in pretty good shape," he said. "One end is worm-eaten and will have to be replaced, but the rest of it is fine." I asked him to proceed.

Several weeks later, I went to get it. He took me to the back of his workshop and there, on an old table, lay the ox yoke. The peeling whitewash was gone and the hard rich golden maple, marbled with black, gleamed. I was amazed.

"Tell me," I asked. "What makes the wood black in places?"

"The sweat of the ox over many years," he explained.

"How did the person who made this get the round shape of the two yokes?"

"With patience, perseverance, pressure, and time," he said. "He took a small, straight maple sapling, poured water on it, bent it a fraction of an inch, and then applied pressure to keep it curved. The next day he did it again, and bent it a bit more. He repeated the process every day until the tree was bowed almost double into a yoke. Sometimes the person making a yoke would wrap the wood in a water-soaked deer skin to keep it wet because if the wood got dried out, it would break."

That ox yoke hangs in our home between the hall and the living room. To me, it is priceless. A friend pointed out that one of the yokes is bigger than the other. He said that was because a farmer would always pair a mature, trained ox with a younger ox-in-training. He added that it was a wonderful picture of how a strong and mature Lord yokes Himself to us in order to help and train us.

As I've been writing about the truths God has repeatedly reminded me of over the years, my brother-in-law's gift has been a metaphor for how God teaches and transforms us. Like the farmer with a young sapling, God uses patience, perseverance, pressure, and time to shape our lives. With patience and perseverance, He causes and controls the pressure—not enough to break the small tree of our spirit, but enough to shape it to become what He wants it to be. And God in His love will take as much time as He knows we need in order to be molded and conformed to the image of His Son.

I'm grateful that God doesn't get weary of the shaping process. But I do—often. It's as though I'm constantly saying, "Come again, Lord? What was that You said? Oh, yes. Now I remember!"

You and I may get impatient with ourselves for not learning more quickly. But let's not get discouraged! Our Father understands that spiritual growth and transformation is a process.

Will you pray with me that we will greet new opportunities to relearn old lessons with anticipation and joy? After all, the Master Yoke-Maker is conforming us for the awesome purpose of being yoked together with Him, for His glory and service.

Though you and I learn slowly, God cares enough for us to remind us again and again of precious lessons. *So, remind me again, Lord. I forget!*

> Now we see but a poor reflection as in a mirror;
> then we shall see face to face.
> Now I know in part; then I shall know fully,
> even as I am fully known.
>
> 1 CORINTHIANS 13:12

# Appendix

*How to Study the Topics in This Book*

Throughout this book I've included study questions to help you explore further what God has to say about each of the topics I address. Though I've supplied questions to get you started, you can do your own inductive study using the following method. I recommend the outline below—an acrostic that spells T-O-P-I-C-A-L—which you can use to study any topic. To help you, I've illustrated this method by outlining the topic of being a servant.

*T is for Title.* (Example: Servanthood)

*O is for Outline.* Look up between twenty and twenty-five verses in a good concordance, and then outline them. (One good outlining method is to answer the questions, who? what? where? how? when? and why?)

Example:
I. Definition of a servant:
   Webster's: One who serves. To exert oneself continuously or statedly for; to obey and worship.
II. Whom are we to serve?
   A. The Lord God. (Deuteronomy 6:13, "Fear the Lord your God; serve him only…")
   B. The Lord Jesus. (Colossians 3:24, "It is the Lord Christ you are serving.")
   C. Others. (Galatians 5:13, "Rather, serve one another in love.")

III. Who are servants?

We are all servants; it is a matter of whom one serves. (Romans 6:16: "Don't you know that when you offer yourselves to someone to obey him as slaves, you are slaves to the one whom you obey—whether you are slaves to sin, which leads to death, or to obedience, which leads to righteousness?")

IV. Characteristics of a servant.

    A. Obedience. (Colossians 3:22: "Slaves, obey your earthly masters in everything; and do it, not only when their eye is on you and to win their favor, but with sincerity of heart and reverence for the Lord" and 1 Peter 2:18: "Submit yourselves to your masters with all respect.")

    B. Humility and respect. (Titus 2:9: "Be subject... to try to please them, not to talk back to them.")

    C. Honesty and faithfulness. (Titus 2:10: "not to steal...but to show that they can be fully trusted.")

V. The heart attitude of one who serves.

    A. Perfect heart. (1 Chronicles 28:9: "Acknowledge the God of your father, and serve him with wholehearted devotion and with a willing mind.")

    B. Singleness of purpose and heart. (Ephesians 6:5-7: "Obey your earthly masters with respect and fear, and with sincerity of heart, just as you would obey Christ...like slaves of Christ, doing the will of God from your heart. Serve wholeheartedly, as if you were serving the Lord, not men.")

    C. Doing it joyfully as to the Lord and not to men. (Preceding verses.)

VI. Results of being a good servant
   A. God is honored. (1 Timothy 6:1: "All who are under the yoke of slavery should consider their masters worthy of full respect, so that God's name and our teaching may not be slandered.")
   B. We will serve God in glory. (Revelation 22:3: "And his servants will serve him.")
VII. Christ is our example.
   Luke 22:27: "I am among you as one who serves."

*P is for Problems.* Jot down any questions or difficulties that the verses bring to mind.

Example: What do you think about the fact that we are all servants of something? What should a servant look like? What should the heart attitude of a servant be? What are the results of being a good servant—now and for eternity? How would you relate the role of servant specifically to women and to wives? How do we become good servants? Can we become a good servant all at once? Is the first step in becoming a servant committing ourselves to the one we are serving? Then what?

*I is for Illustrations.* Come up with some illustrations from your reading or experience.

Example: From the Bible, Joseph in Genesis 39 serving Potiphar; the servant of Abraham sent to get a wife for Isaac in Genesis 24.

*C is for Commentaries.* Look up the topic in a good commentary and add to your insight. (This should be AFTER you've done your own original thinking.)

*A is for Application.* This is the most important part. Select one verse or passage that God is speaking to you about and then apply it to yourself.

Example: Ephesians 6:5-7.

1. Write out the verse in your own words.

Servants, the people you serve are to be obeyed respectfully and sincerely, just as you would obey Christ. And this obedience isn't just to win favor when they are watching, but should be done like you'd obey God—from the heart. You should serve people with your whole heart as though you are doing it for God.

2. Write out how you've failed to obey this verse.

Rarely do I think about serving. Too often I just want everything and everyone to serve me. (The weather should be good, the planes should be on time, the clerks should be polite and helpful, and my husband should bring me breakfast in bed!)

3. Give a specific illustration of a failure to have a servant attitude. Be as current as possible.

Yesterday I grew irritated when no one at the gas station came to help me put air in my tires. Why? I expected them to serve me.

4. Write out specific steps you feel God would have you take to put this verse into practice THIS WEEK. (Ideas: Memorize the verse, put it at the top of your prayer list.)

This week I will memorize two verses on servanthood. I will ask God to show me the times I demand that people serve me as well as areas where I can serve others. I will also look for one way each day to specifically serve someone—preferably in a way I don't usually serve.

5. If at all possible, have someone check up on your progress.

This will be difficult! But I'll ask Jack to point out to me when I'm not acting like a servant.

*L is for List.* Keep a list of verses to memorize in the future.

• Colossians 3:23-24

- 1 Timothy 6:1
- Galatians 5:13

May God deepen your walk with Him as you dig into His Word for precious reminders of invaluable truths.

# NOTES

**Chapter One: "He Loves Me"**

1. See Colossians 3:3.

**Chapter Four: Amazing Grace**

1. See Judges 6–7.

**Chapter Eight: "Yes, But…"**

1. J. D. Douglass, ed., *New Bible Dictionary*, 2nd ed. (Wheaton, Ill.: Tyndale, 1985), 428.

2. *Hymns for the Family of God*, "It Is Well with My Soul," words by Horatio Spafford, music by Philip Bliss (Nashville, Tenn.: Paragon Associates, Inc., 1976), 495.

**Chapter Sixteen: When "Enough" Is Enough**

1. Randy Alcorn, *Dominion* (Sisters, Ore.: Multnomah, 1997), 14.

2. See Matthew 9:18-25; 9:27-30; 15:21-28.

3. See Matthew 14:13-21; Mark 5:1-20; John 9:1-11; John 11:1-44; Mark 4:35-41; Luke 7:11-16; John 5:1-15.

**Chapter Seventeen: Holy Ground**

1. See Leviticus 21; Numbers 4:35.

**Chapter Twenty: Little Foxes**

1. Lorraine Pintus, "At Peace in the Whirlwind," *Discipleship Journal*, no. 97 (1997): 62.

2. See Philippians 2:3; 1 Peter 5:6.

## Chapter Twenty-One: "All" Means "All"

1. Amy Carmichael, *Edges of His Ways* (Fort Washington, Penn.: Christian Literature Crusade, 1955), 8.

2. Quoted in Anne Ortlund, *I Want to See You, Lord* (Eugene, Ore.: Harvest House, 1997), 196, 175.

## Chapter Twenty-Two: From Glum to Glad

1. Dawson Trotman, founder of the Navigators, was in charge of Glen Eyrie at the time.

## Chapter Twenty-Four: Count It All Joy

1. Frank E. Gaebelein, *The Expositor's Bible Commentary*, vol. 11 (Grand Rapids, Mich.: Zondervan, 1978), 291.

2. Paul Thigpen, "Where's the Joy?" *Discipleship Journal*, no. 93 (1996): 19.

## Chapter Twenty-Eight: Whom Do You Serve?

1. Ruth Harms Calkin, "I Wonder," in *Tell Me Again, Lord, I Forget* (Carol Stream, Ill.: Tyndale, 1974), 14. Used by permission. All rights reserved.

## Chapter Thirty-Two: Forgiveness Is Not a Feeling

1. David Augsburger, *Cherishable: Love and Marriage* (Scottdale, Penn.: Herald, 1973), 143.

2. Steve and Annie Chapman, *Married Lovers, Married Friends* (Minneapolis, Minn.: Bethany, 1989), 62.

## Chapter Thirty-Three: "Jump; I'll Catch You!"

1. Dianne Hales, "Three Words That Heal," *Readers Digest,* June 1994, 61.

2. Ron Mehl, *Meeting God at a Dead End* (Sisters, Ore.: Multnomah, 1996), 91.

## Chapter Thirty-Five: Humble Adoration

1. Steven J. Lawson, *Heaven Help Us!* (Colorado Springs, Colo.: NavPress, 1995), 62.
2. Lawson, *Heaven Help Us!* 61-2.
3. Warren and Ruth Myers, "The Joy in Humility," *Discipleship Journal*, no. 105: 34.

## Chapter Thirty-Six: Is Your Container Ready?

1. See Exodus 32.
2. Anne Ortlund, *I Want to See You, Lord* (Eugene, Ore.: Harvest House, 1998), 12.
3. Ortlund, *I Want to See You, Lord,* 25.

## Chapter Thirty-Eight: The Refining Process

1. David Roper, *Seeing Through* (Sisters, Ore.: Multnomah, 1995), 88.